Bankism

How the Government's Bank-First
Policies are Destroying the Nation and
How to Survive the Aftermath of a
Coming Dollar Collapse

BILL BODRI

Top Shape Publishing, LLC
1135 Terminal Way #209
Reno, Nevada 89502

ISBN-10: 0-9980764-6-5
ISBN-13: 978-0-9980764-6-1
Library of Congress Number: 2017914575

The purpose of the book is to stimulate thought and enquiry and is not investment advice. No methodology is promising you profits of any type. Neither the author or publisher make any representations about the suitability of the information contained in the book and all information is provided "as is" without warranty of any kind. This book is sold with the understanding that the publisher and author are not engaged in rendering legal, accounting, securities trading, investment advising or other professional services. It does not provide investment advice because the author has no knowledge of the specific investment objectives or financial circumstances and specific needs of any individual reading it. The author and publisher do NOT accept liability for any investment decisions (profits and losses incurred) by you based on the ideas, information, discussions, software, courses, and websites referenced within. All readers must obtain expert investment advice from qualified professionals before committing funds.

DEDICATION

This book is dedicated to helping you survive and profit from the troubled waters ahead caused by Bankism, which has been the government's misguided policy to put the importance of banks above the public welfare. America has experienced the destruction of its manufacturing base, the offshoring of its Middle Class jobs, a bold attempt to stimulate its economy through mortgage booms and toxic debt, massive banking system and central bank overextension and insolvency, the crumbling of the Petrodollar, and Eurasian moves to replace US dollar institutions and bypass the dollar in world trade. Our economic future is now imperiled because of gross mismanagement by America's financial powers. Our standard of living has been artificially propped up to unsustainable heights by massive amounts of fiat money that will evaporate soon. Here is a history of what brought us to this precarious state of affairs, the key actors involved, what most probably lies ahead and how to protect yourself from the coming consequences.

CONTENTS

ACKNOWLEDGMENTS

This book owes a debt to the many sources reporting on the great destruction caused by Bankism and subsequent the financialization of the economy it has engendered. Many people have chronicled the catastrophic loss of American manufacturing and destruction caused by the offshoring of American jobs for corporate profits. They have also warned about the potential collapse of the Petrodollar, which will wreak financial havoc within America. My debt extends to the websites reporting on the *real news* of the nation such as this. I therefore wish to thank the many financial analysts and commentators who have tirelessly worked to publicize these economic dangers and what the monetary authorities have brought upon us through the reckless policies of Bankism that have risked the dollar by preferring banks over the broader economy and public in general. Our failed monetary policy has created and preserved dysfunctional banks while wrecking the greater U.S. economy. As Kuan Tzu once said, the best bank is to store the country's wealth among its people but that is not what we have been doing. Impoverishing people and business simply in order to keep banks alive rather than reorganize them has not lead to the highest welfare of the nation but to catastrophe. The coming collapse of the dollar and decay of the US dollar sphere, whenever it occurs, is tied to all these trends.

1
THE FEDERAL RESERVE

The United States has a central bank called the Federal Reserve, which is usually called the "Fed" for short.

Kevin Warsh, a Fed governor from 2006 to 2011, recently said publicly, "The Fed is the nation's third experiment with a central bank, and the reason it's our third is because the first two didn't go so well."

With that simple history as a guide, one should therefore assume that the present Federal Reserve banking system has not been granted the boon of perpetuity either. It may eventually lose its way, just like its forbears, so as to eventually require a restructuring or total replacement.

The present Federal Reserve system began in a project created in November 1910 when six men – Nelson Aldrich, A. Piatt Andrew, Henry Davison, Arthurs Shelton, Frank Vanderlip and Paul Warburg, secretly met off the coast of Georgia on Jekyll Island to write a plan to reform the U.S. banking system.

The framework of the initial plan slowly morphed into the Federal Reserve Act that made the US dollar a fiat currency backed by the taxing authority of the U.S. government. There was strong opposition to the proposed

Federal Reserve Act even from bankers, but Congress passed it and the President signed the act in December 1913. It set up the Federal Reserve not as a government agency but as a corporation that was chartered by the federal government instead of the states.

At present, there is public confusion about the fact that the Federal Reserve is not a government agency. It is actually a privately owned institution whose stockholders are private banks. Most of the U.S. population doesn't know that at its core the Fed is a private banking organization with private stockholders. The fact that its shareholders are banks perhaps explains why its many actions usually favor the profits of member banks at the expense of the public good. The public relations rationale always provided is that helping the banks is helping the economy and thus is helping the public, but is that always true?

Even though the twelve regional Federal Reserve banks are named using the word "federal," not a single one is a federal institution whose beneficiary is the public. They are all independent, privately owned and locally controlled corporations (Lewis v. United States, 680 F.2d 1239 (1982), the United States Court of Appeals, Ninth Circuit).

Want more proof other than legal rulings?

Consider the fact that Federal Reserve employees are not part of the U.S. Civil Service system. Federal Reserve banks are not listed as government organizations by the telephone companies either. Unlike federal government organizations, Federal Reserve banks also pay their own postage like any other corporation. In fact, no part of the U.S. government pays Fed bills and determines its budget. The Fed basically gets its money by engaging in "open market operations." The physical property of Federal Reserve banks is also held privately and is subject to local taxation whereas government property is not.

You must also consider that the Federal Reserve has stockholders whereas no Federal agency has nor should have stockholders. Everything federal is supposed to be owned by the public whereas the Federal Reserve is not. To make matters even more clear, by law Federal Reserve stockholders receive an annual dividend of 6%.

Having stockholders with dividends, the Fed is most definitely a private corporation with owners. When the Fed was founded the original stockholders included the largest banks of the U.S., but because of mergers and acquisitions you cannot trace with perfect clarity who actually owns its stock today. The private banking owners of the Fed, its true shareholders, are a closely guarded secret. The only truth we know with certainty about their identity is that the U.S. government owns zero shares.

The Federal Reserve Board of Governors, on the other hand, is considered an entirely federal agency (Kennedy C. Scott vs. Federal Reserve Bank of Kansas City (2005), the U.S. Court of Appeals, Eighth Circuit). Strange, however, is the fact that only in 2015 did the Federal Reserve finally change its website from .org to .gov, which begs the question why this took so long and what the change actually means.

The .gov domain name is restricted to government entities, but other Federal Reserve entities, such as the Federal Reserve member banks (the Federal Reserve Bank of Boston, New York, Philadelphia, Cleveland, Richmond, Atlanta, Chicago, St. Louis, Minneapolis, Kansas City, Dallas, and San Francisco) retain the .org domain name in their websites, thus confirming that they are not in any way government agencies, but private entities.

Adding to the ambiguity, the Federal Reserve Board, in the Frequently Asked Questions section on its website, once wrote, "The Federal Reserve System is not 'owned' by anyone and is not a private, profit-making institution. Instead, it is an independent entity within the government, having both public purposes and private aspects. ..." This is worded in such a way as to confirm that the Fed is not owned by individuals (without ruling out corporate shareholders) and is a quasi-government agency without actually being a government agency. It is kind of a hybrid organization that has some characteristics of government and some characteristics of a private corporation, but is neither purely. It is independent of government, which is one of the reasons it was created in the first place. For instance, the Federal Reserve decisions do not have to be ratified by any branches of government.

The primary motivation for creating the Federal Reserve system was to create a "lender of last resort" to address banking panics. Its original mandate was to help keep the private banking system intact during dangerous financial situations. Since it is not a federal agency it receives funding via an annual 6% dividend of monopolistic profits paid to Federal Reserve shareholder banks.

The Federal Reserve also has a monetary policy mandate dating back to The Federal Reserve Act of 1977. This mandate is that the Fed should work to establish "maximum employment, stable prices and moderate long-term interest rates" in the nation. The actual wording of the monetary policy objective is that "The Board of Governors of the Federal Reserve System and the Federal Open Market Committee shall maintain long run growth of the monetary and credit aggregates commensurate with the economy's long run potential to increase production, so as to promote effectively the goals of maximum employment, stable prices, and moderate long-term interest rates."

This sounds great, so does it mean that the Federal Reserve acts in the public interest as its primary objective? Despite this mandate, after carefully evaluating its track record the conclusion you must come to is no. Rather, while "following the guidelines" the Fed primarily acts in the interest of the banking system so as to *maintain its profitability*. That is its first and foremost priority. It has allowed a private banking cartel of the nation's largest banks to join together and control their own industry by preventing competition and making sure they have secure profit margins through their own banking regulations. Banks have even been saved from bankruptcy at taxpayers' cost.

The historical norm is that monetary or banking cartels typically establish a stranglehold that eventually destroys the economic basis of the nation, like a parasite that grows and prospers until it kills its host. Banking cartels typically cause some type of monetary destruction in their desire for monopolistic profits, destroy their hosts and then die as a result.

The United States is the host for the Federal Reserve banking cartel and is presently staggering under a tremendous load of debt it has issued in order to save the U.S. banking system from excesses the Fed created. The Federal Reserve cannot take on more debt, nor can it truly raise interest rates on a debt load already near $100 trillion, a mind-boggling amount that can never be paid back. Raising interest rates would kill the economy and the financial lattice work structure that is holding everything in place via extensive networks of derivatives contracts. Since a staggering debt that cannot be repaid will not be repaid, default is in the inevitable future. Due to the actions of the Federal Reserve in mismanaging U.S. monetary policy, the U.S. is financially handcuffed and at the door of bankruptcy unable to move away from a coming calamity. Even the status of the Petrodollar is at stake.

While intelligent American forces no doubt are quietly maneuvering to create a new system similar to the old one we now have, which will surely suffer from an inevitable collapse, there is one especially positive solution that can replace the system in a praiseworthy fashion when it finally goes belly up.

Countries which at one time had central banks that were completely owned by the government, such as Japan and Germany, became so economically strong (from release of the debt load) that their prosperity threatened other countries in the world. They grew in strength because they issued currency without debt and so were free of shackling interest payments. If an economic collapse ever occurs in the world, returning to this type of structure would be an absolutely necessary part of the cure for repairing and rebooting the system. The progress of a country, and even a civilization, will relate to the degree to which it is free from the influence of debt and we must use this fact to reboot the financial system if a collapse ever comes.

The U.S. Treasury used to be the nation's central bank, but the Federal Reserve broke the Treasury off to put money creation into the hands of Wall Street. We have to put the Treasury in control of money creation once again. If the Fed were disbanded or to become a true federal agency because the U.S. owned its central bank, then the U.S. government could issue U.S. legal tender directly rather than having the Fed issue it as a private debt to the banking system. This would actually benefit taxpayers (rather than the Federal Reserve banks) not just because of the lower costs but because the government would lend quite differently than banks, which tend to favor loans to mergers and acquisitions, stock buy-backs, and to inflate real estate prices. In charge of money creation, the government could lend to local and state governments interest-free, thus dramatically cutting the price of public projects like infrastructure.

As demonstrated in *The Public Bank Solution* by Ellen Brown, history definitely shows that countries which used this system became the most powerful economic hegemons of their time because they freed their economies from the shackles of unnecessary debt. This is part of the solution when the Federal Reserve must one day face the reckoning of "being reorganized" as has happened twice before in the past.

2
THE EXCHANGE
STABILIZATION FUND

The Fed is the best known, but not the *only* organization conducting U.S. monetary operations. There is also the Exchange Stabilization Fund (ESF), which most people have never even heard of. The ESF is a super-secretive Treasury department operation created by the Gold Reserve Act of 1934 to protect the value of the dollar. It does so primarily by buying and selling foreign currency. To defend the value of the dollar it is frequently involved in massive foreign currency interventions.

This mandate of protecting the dollar is related to the maintenance of the Petrodollar system as the sole payment standard for the world's oil trade. Protecting the US dollar is also connected with the national security objective of maintaining its status as the world's reserve currency.

Whatever world activities threaten the use of the Petrodollar in the global oil trade or the dollar's status as the world's reserve currency imperil the implicit value of the US dollar. Thus those activities, whatever they might be, always attract the attention of the ESF and its operational arms. History also clearly documents that the ESF has had close connections with the CIA and has paid for a number of extraneous activities involving other countries. The historical evidence is clear that the ESF has become and will become involved in whatever is relevant to its mandate of protecting the dollar, whether that involves regime change, arms deals or whatever. With the CIA's involvement some speculate this may even extend to assassinations, blackmail, bribery, drugs and more.

In addition to performing foreign currency operations, such as promoting exchange rate stability and countering disorderly conditions in foreign exchange markets, the ESF is also the official channel for the U.S. Treasury's gold dealings. It is thought to be one of the hidden parties that regularly puts downward price pressure on the price of gold via the naked selling of tens of thousands of COMEX exchange contracts during the most weakly traded hours of the market. Suppressing the price of gold, interfering with the price discovery mechanism, is an activity that benefits the dollar by helping to maintain its value, which helps explain why gold is one of the most heavily manipulated (namely suppressed) commodity markets.

Lastly, the ESF is a major conduit by which the U.S. Treasury gives aid to foreign countries, namely loans to foreign governments *without* need of Congressional approval. The ESF is the one who makes the loans.

Extremely powerful but well hidden, most people have never even heard of the ESF, which the Treasury calls its funding arm. This opaqueness mirrors the fact that the public is also not perfectly clear about the private quasi-government status of the Federal Reserve system either. The ESF is even more covert, including the fact that its 1934 inception basically hijacked many of the powers of the Fed and that over time it has basically captured the Fed bureaucracy.

By law, it is not the Federal Reserve but the Secretary of the Treasury who is actually the chief international monetary policy maker of the United States, so in international monetary affairs the Fed takes its directions from the U.S. Treasury. Hence, operations in *international finance* are actually controlled by the U.S. Treasury, not the Federal Reserve, and some are executed through the ESF. Treasury interventions extend to bailouts of foreign banks or companies, foreign currency swaps or derivatives, and various currency market operations. Although it should be the province of the Fed, even changes in the trend of U.S. interest rates seem to regularly occur whenever an individual becomes the new Secretary of the Treasury.

Under the Secretary of the Treasury's control, ESF operations are conducted through the New York Fed, which operates as its executive trading arm. Therefore it is from within the New York Federal Reserve Bank, acting as its clearing agent, that the ESF conducts its trading activities and exerts control over international finance. The New York Fed, acting on the behalf of the ESF by serving as its front, thereby camouflages the ESF's foreign trading interventions to defend the dollar. In other words, the Federal Reserve is the prime broker for the ESF and takes the heat for any real world interventions that are actually due to the ESF. An accurate audit of the Fed would no doubt show this, which is another of the many reasons that the Fed does not want to be audited.

The ESF is actually the largest and most powerful financial agency in the world, but its covert operations keep it extremely well-hidden. Credit and blame are usually apportioned to the Fed for its activities; anything that the Federal Reserve does on the ESF's behalf does not officially happen including currency trades in forwards, swaps, derivative transactions and other manipulations. While the Fed comes before Congress twice a year for oversight, the ESF reports to no one and thus its activities remain unmonitored.

The ESF is part of the executive branch and thus free of congressional controls and not subject to legislative oversight. No government office informs Congress of any of the non-monetary activities funded by the ESF, including foreign loans or other foreign interventions. As you might infer, the ability to keep Congress in the dark naturally leads to the potential for mammoth abuse.

Due to the Gold Reserve Act of 1934, the U.S. Treasury was given powers that emasculated the Federal Reserve's powers set up in 1913. By this Act the Treasury was enabled to use the ESF to buy or sell gold, foreign currencies, securities, and other financial instruments in order to control the dollar's value. It could then conduct open-market operations without the assistance or approval of the Federal Reserve. Section 12 of the Act authorized the president to establish the gold value of the dollar by proclamation, which President Roosevelt did the day after he signed the Act. At that time, Roosevelt explained that his purpose was to increase the supply of credit, "to stabilize domestic prices and to protect the foreign commerce against the adverse effect of depreciated foreign currencies."

At that time, the *Washington Post* (whose publisher, Eugene Meyer, had been governor of the Federal Reserve Board) wrote that by this Act the Federal Reserve was deprived of its power to formulate an independent credit policy and could no longer regulate the flow of funds into and out of the country. This was a power it had had when the United States was on the gold standard. By this Act the central banking system formally surrendered one of the chief privileges, powers and duties that it had exercised prior to the suspension of gold payments.

With the passage of 1934 Gold Reserve Act, therefore, the executive Administration assumed responsibility for defining our monetary policies. The Act shifted control of monetary powers from Federal Reserve to the Treasury in the main areas where power mattered, thus giving the U.S. Treasury control over the Federal Reserve in those arenas. The Secretary of the Treasury could effectively nullify anything the Fed did, and the Treasury's actions started to affect domestic credit conditions. If the Fed was in control of interest rates rather than the Treasury then the appointment of a new Secretary of the Treasury would never affect interest rate trends, but historical charts prove that this certainly happens with consistency.

One particular problem is that the Secretary of Treasury often has had very little banking experience, yet has incredible power in his management of ESF interventions. Since the ESF is basically an unreviewable authority without oversight that engages in covert international finance actions, in essence the Secretary of Treasury (via the ESF) has dictatorial powers of nearly unlimited financial authority, allowing him to operate international financial affairs out of the view of Congress.

For instance, the first ever GAO audit of the Federal Reserve revealed that $16 trillion had been secretly given out to U.S. financial entities *and foreign banks* between December 2007 and June 2010. In other words, the Federal Reserve secretly bailed out many of the world's banks, corporations and governments. But were these Federal Reserve bailouts or the workings of the ESF? Some of the institutions receiving bailout funds include the following:

Citigroup: $2.5 trillion
Morgan Stanley: $2.04 trillion
Merrill Lynch: $1.949 trillion
Bank of America: $1.344 trillion
Barclays PLC (United Kingdom): $868 billion
Bear Sterns: $853 billion
Goldman Sachs: $814 billion
Royal Bank of Scotland (UK): $541 billion
JP Morgan Chase: $391 billion
Deutsche Bank (Germany): $354 billion
UBS (Switzerland): $287 billion
Credit Suisse (Switzerland): $262 billion

Lehman Brothers: $183 billion
Bank of Scotland (United Kingdom): $181 billion
BNP Paribas (France): $175 billion

While these bailouts appear on the books of the Federal Reserve, by law this should have been (and may actually have been) an ESF Treasury operation executed by the offices of the Fed. The point is that the Secretary of Treasury has no obligations to report on his management of the ESF which few have ever heard of, and which has been used as a U.S. secret weapon in many international affairs.

The ESF, as stated, is reputed to have had a hand in financing many secretive CIA operations across the world that were intended to advance U.S. interests. If it must become involved with criminal enterprise to exercise its mandate of supporting the dollar then some say the ESF will do so. Because of its powers and (supposed) adherence to its mandate, the ESF can and has been consistently used as a source of funds for projects, even covert operations, that escape Congressional oversight and approval. Some have speculated that ESF attempts to defend the dollar may even involve war to eliminate any US dollar rivals, especially when there are threats that might end its reign as the world's reserve currency.

The ESF has never been investigated, so the public and even Congress doesn't precisely know what it has actually done (including the exact details of many international bailouts and foreign loan arrangements other than those appearing in the GAO audit) since no one has ever asked questions. Most people don't even know that it exists. Neither does anyone know the extent to which the ESF has global operational tentacles with the ability to rig, corrupt or control many world financial markets. The world only knows about the Plunge Protection Team ("Working Group") composed of the SEC, Fed, Treasury and Commodity Futures Trading Commission that props up the stock market during downturns, but has no idea of the actual operations undertaken by the ESF and how it commonly intervenes to control countless world markets. It is one of the secret super weapons of the United States.

In essence, without oversight the ESF actually operates with a self-appointed mission. Its dollar mandate puts its involvement at the highest levels of national security and thus it commonly masks its activities to render them invisible. It even goes so far as to fudge or obfuscate various government statistics related to its efforts so as not to alert or frighten the public about the issues and dangers it normally deals with.

WHY ALL THE CONCERN?

What dangers could possibly require the rapt attention and clandestine efforts of this super-secretive U.S. along with the CIA?

Here is the fact that the average American newscaster, politician, academic and even citizen is ignorant about. The foremost objective of U.S. geopolitical strategy is to maintain the US dollar's standing as the world's reserve currency and as the predominant currency used for transacting world trade. To maintain its value, the US dollar needs to maintain its importance in (1) world banking reserves and (2) global trade payments. Maintaining the dollar's standing in these two areas is a primary objective of U.S. geopolitical strategy.

The greenback has held its position as global reserve currency since the end of World War II. It now accounts for 60% of global banking reserves and 80% of global payments, but those numbers are always changing. For instance, China conducts more global trade than any other nation, but the renminbi only accounts for about 10% of global trade. This figure will surely increase in the future.

For the U.S. to maintain its status in world trade requires that most countries continue using the dollar to buy oil since petroleum transactions constitute a major proportion of global trade. Since the money flows involved with illegal drugs are enormous too, it is also important that (until eliminated) the dollar is used as the main go-between for the illegal global narcotics trafficking as well.

This dominant status of the US dollar in world trade keeps the largest U.S. banks afloat with dollar currency flows and makes many other strategic hegemon programs possible. Without the Petrodollar's status in the world oil trade, the demand for dollars would plummet worldwide and the United States would have to change all its tax, debt, currency, trade, military and energy policies. For instance, the U.S. Congress would not be able to raise the U.S. debt limit indefinitely because the global demand for dollars, which usually finances that debt, would decrease dramatically. The value of gold, globally priced in dollars, would also likely rise.

If foreign countries suddenly did not need to use the dollar in trade transactions, foreign countries would dump the dollar for some alternative. Global banking systems would suffer shockwaves due to the tectonic consequences this would entail. No longer would they buy U.S. Treasury bonds and bills to park the dollars they previously required for international trade. Global money flows would tilt toward the new alternative trading vehicle, which might be a currency (such as the renminbi), a cryptocurrency, gold or even a gold-backed cryptocurrency. Eventually real assets, like gold, will indeed be cryptoized.

If the dollar lost its status as the global trade payments vehicle or as the world's reserve currency, the loss of power and prestige are not the only problems the U.S. would face. If this happened the Federal Reserve would lose its unfettered ability to print dollars to solve domestic economic problems. Domestic interest rates in America would rise sharply, adjustable rate mortgage holders would be crushed and real estate values would plummet. Domestic financial asset prices would tumble too. Import prices would skyrocket (sometimes even doubling if the dollar devalues by 50%), and shortages would hit the U.S. supply chain. Businesses would collapse nationwide and massive layoffs would ensue. Unemployment would explode and entitlement spending would be at risk. Americans would quickly find themselves in Third World living conditions. Standards of living would drastically plunge. The U.S. would enter into a crippling depression and be forced to massively contract its military machine. Its entire monetary system would have to be rejiggered.

Without being able to finance its various policies and military forays simply by printing dollars, the global hegemonic powers of the U.S. would be absolutely demolished, perhaps curtailed completely. Economically the U.S. would probably experience a depression with an eventual recovery at a new normal with far lower living standards.

These issues are so critically vital to U.S. interests that you will never hear of them in the news, but one is not really qualified to be a statesman if they don't know about these *real* issues. There is the face that the government puts on matters in order to deal with the public, and the real truth that it secretly deals with behind closed doors. There are always the ostensible or apparent *surface reasons* provided to people to make policies acceptable, and then there are the *real reasons* why things are done in geopolitics. As to the concern for the US dollar, the fear that the US dollar's usage will decline due to some other country's activities explains many of America's interventions in nations abroad. This is what most of our foreign wars are really about, namely maintaining the value of the US dollar.

Other than a currency collapse, there are other types of financial and monetary risk that can also destroy a nation's economy. This includes monetary system structural changes, sovereign debt defaults, banking system defaults, and hyperinflation. With the dollar in decline, these risks will rise.

For instance, every 30-40 years the reigning monetary system of the world usually fails, bringing with it tremendous changes, and then it has to be retooled to start again. Over the last century the world monetary system has already collapsed three times – in 1914, again in 1939 and most recently in 1971 when Nixon ended the Bretton Woods agreement by going off the gold standard – so another collapse would not be unusual at all.

Each time the monetary system collapsed it wasn't the end of the world, nonetheless this type of event is something that the Fed and ESF worries about. There is always an eventual end to these types of crisis because people absolutely need some form of money as a unit of exchange. Therefore there is always an end to any turmoil when a new normal is established because commerce never stops. The world powers always turn to something new that reboots the entire system, but the question for us is whether the next reboot, which will surely occur, will still involve the US dollar as the center of operations. The answer is probably no.

Sovereign debt defaults are a smaller issue than a global monetary rejiggering because they usually involve just one nation. Reinhart and Rogoff did a study on sovereign debt defaults and found that since 1800 there have been approximately 250 cases globally where governments have defaulted on their debt. The immediately preceding cause has usually been a banking crisis that typically leads to the sovereign debt default, which in turn typically leads to inflation (greater than 20% per year) and then currency collapse.

As to currency collapses, history also shows that the average life expectancy for a fiat currency is less than 40 years. Throughout history fiat currencies (paper currencies not backed by commodities such as oil or gold) have had nearly a 100% failure rate. This is not a track record that provides optimism for the future of the US dollar. Rather, it should serve as the acknowledgment of a ticking time bomb.

Since most currencies have lasted no longer than the average human lifespan, you should expect to see a major currency failure or reengineering effort that affects you during your life. Given enough time, eventually all fiat currencies fail and therefore it is only a question of time and circumstances for this to happen to any country, including the United States. Political systems always eventually abuse a currency (usually by debasing it to death), and a country always eventually pays the price. That is, the citizens of a country always pay the price for the abuse of a financial system caused by its government.

Let us review the facts to be sure. A study of 775 fiat currencies by DollarDaze.org reported that 21% were destroyed by war, 20% failed through hyperinflation, 12% were destroyed through independence, 24% had to be monetarily reformed, and 23% were still in circulation awaiting one of these outcomes. Researcher Vince Cate researched the fate of 599 dead paper currencies and found that 28% were destroyed by war, 15% ended through acts of national independence (the new states renamed or reissued new currency), 30% ended through monetary unions or reforms (such as the creation of the Euro) and 27% were destroyed by hyperinflation.

Hyperinflation is one of the possible events that can destroy a currency. Hyperinflation is not some fairy tale fable that never occurs, but a real risk to modern nations. One need only turn to the current cases of Venezuela and Zimbabwe to see it presently in action.

Peter Bernholtz, author of *Monetary Regimes and Inflation*, found that most every case of hyperinflation was first caused by massive budget deficits that were financed in large regard by excessive money creation (such as what we are seeing in the U.S. today). The money printing finally caused hyperinflation after a specific tipping point.

The historical tipping point to hyperinflation has usually come when government deficits reached 40% or more of *government spending* (not GDP). Hyperinflation is practically a surety when debt rises to over 80% of GDP and deficits amount to more than 40% of government spending, *no matter how a country got into that situation.* During a hyperinflation practically the only thing that can save you are investments in the precious metals (gold and silver) or holding other currencies immune to its effects.

Hyperinflations have historically been caused by legislatures that spent far beyond their means and thereby racked up a debt load that became disproportionately large relative to the economy. Unfunded liabilities usually grew so much that even with severe budget cuts, which we now call "austerity," the government could no longer tax its way out of the situation. This lead to even more money printing, inflation and then an eventual loss of faith in the currency followed by collapse.

If a country keeps recklessly inflating its currency without limit through endless money printing or bond issuance, people commonly lose faith and confidence in that currency when they discover what has been happening. Then they will dump the currency, rendering it worthless and paving the way for hyperinflation.

Can this really happen to the United States? It has already happened during the American Revolutionary War!

No one wants to hold onto an asset that is declining in value, so a national paper currency (or government bonds) will be dumped en masse when people find that it has been printed into oblivion for some reason. You cannot keep printing money, keep interest rates low and have your currency stay strong forever. To think you can do this forever is simply insanity.

Consider this. Printing money cannot produce prosperity otherwise everyone would simply do it without limit. There must be negative consequences to money printing. Eventually your currency will drop in value, and if the government then keeps printing currency to pay its bills then you will get hyperinflation, which has happened time and again throughout history. This is the historical pattern. When the national currency ends up becoming worthless then this ends the life of that paper currency.

The typical collapse scenario is usually extremely high inflation after the progressive debasement of the currency through excessive money printing, and then its eventual replacement. This is a type of implicit default that usually leads to larger political changes too.

Having already suffered through the hyperinflation of the Continental dollar, which was printed into oblivion to finance the Revolutionary War, the American founders of the Constitution understood the dangers of fiat currency and a debt-based financial system. Therefore they enshrined specific protections within the Constitution with the intent to prevent future generations from creating this calamity again.

The United States Constitution therefore declares, in Article I, Section 10, "No State shall ... make any Thing but gold and silver Coin a Tender in Payment of Debts." This means that no State can make something besides gold or silver a "tender in payment" for any debts, which effectively prevents hyperinflation. Unfortunately, the United States has long since abandoned any adherence to this principle.

The job of a central bank is to worry. All these possible eventualities are therefore the proper concerns of the Federal Reserve *and* the Exchange Stabilization Fund and they do attract their attention.

Over the past few years the U.S. banking system has been supported by the QE policy of quantitative easing, which has been an extreme case of hypermonetary inflation sure to end badly. How to get out of this mess without destruction is now the daily quandary of U.S. monetary authorities who lay awake at night wondering how to manage a sinking ship.

In basic terms, the U.S. has been monetizing its federal

debt at an extreme rate to keep the banking system solvent while simultaneously trying to maintain the dollar's value and its usage in world trade. Unfortunately for the dollar, QE monetization has so degraded its value that U.S. monetary authorities have turned to massive derivative operations, which artificially fabricate U.S. Treasury bond demand, to maintain its value. The U.S. now has an incredible sum of wealth tied up in worthless paper derivatives whose sole existence is to maintain the value of the dollar and to prop up U.S. Treasury bonds and global oil prices so that the dam doesn't break.

For instance, the Chinese renminbi has become a growing competitor for global trade transactions. As its usage increases worldwide simple arithmetic tells us that the dollar's importance will lessen in global trade payment. Therefore we will eventually see more and more Treasury bond dumping from foreign banks who need to hold the renminbi rather than the US dollar for trade payments. Those same nations will also readily dump the dollar at any moment they feel that the value of their dollar holdings is threatened.

What might domestically threaten the value of the dollar? As historians have pointed out, the risks include extreme levels of money printing and debt levels that might lead to a sovereign debt default, currency collapse or even hyperinflation.

The dollar will definitely undergo a crisis, fast or slow, if its unpopularity leads to massive global rejection. Countries have already been dumping U.S. Treasury bills and bonds at an increasing rate, and hence the alarm has already sounded. The ESF must be vigilant because both it and the Fed will have to become the buyers of last resort if deeper problems occur.

Luckily, the tipping point of collapse has not yet appeared, but the risks are there and finally recognized. What risks? Russia has begun establishing a large oil and gas consortium that will trade the energy sector in non-

USD payments. China has begun replacing the dollar in international trade payments, and is building non-dollar financial platforms that no longer depend on its usage. For a variety of different reasons, foreign nations have also begun to divest themselves of dollar instruments in earnest – namely Treasury bonds and Treasury bills – thus foreshadowing a possible end to the dollar's dominance.

What are the largest global transactional uses of the dollar that are still keeping it afloat? International petroleum sales in dollar terms is the key figure that U.S. financial entities worry about most, although incredibly large dollar sums are also being used in narcotics trafficking. These illegal dollar fund flows are actually keeping the banking systems of many nations afloat, which is one of the reasons why they may never be eradicated. Perhaps the need to control and even maintain these money flows is why the CIA is constantly implicated in the worldwide drug trade.

The honest truth is that the drug trade produces money flows that are just as much defended by war and murder as war and assassinations are used to defend the dollar's necessity in various types of global trade, such as the Petrodollar. *The US dollar is undeniably backed by the war machine since its health is the primary, foremost geopolitical strategic concern of the United States.* Other governments understand this, but the American public does not. The public doesn't have a clue as to the real reasons behind most U.S. military interventions, particularly in Petrodollar nations.

The point is that the ESF is tasked with maintaining the value of the dollar, and there are incredible risks to the fate of the dollar at the moment. Any ESF attempts to defend the dollar essentially include both financial interventions and funding military actions to eliminate any US dollar rivals, especially activities which threaten its status as the world's most popular trading vehicle.

3
THE DEFENSE OF THE PETRODOLLAR

Charged with maintaining the value of the dollar, the ESF sees any reason that might cause an exodus from the US dollar as a threat. It views any trends which abandon the dollar as a risk to the nation.

Maintaining the dollar's usage as the primary payments vehicle for settling world trade is the number one security issue of the United States and the strategic reason why the U.S. continually interferes in the Mideast. If OPEC oil nations started accepting any currency other than the US dollar for oil payments, this might lead to large scale abandonment of the dollar. That would, in turn, plunge the U.S. into Third World nation status. Thus the threat is monitored and steps are taken whenever this status is threatened.

Is this threat over-stated? Consider that the value of the dollar is implicitly backed by the petroleum trade (or one could say "backed by the commodity petroleum") and that the U.S. places its naval carrier groups across the globe at the oceanic choke points regulating ocean petroleum freight. It doesn't do this to guarantee the flow of free trade, but to ensure that nations conduct the petroleum trade using the US dollar. The key for the U.S. is not to abuse the Petrodollar standard by printing trillions more dollars than there is an equivalent amount of oil trade.

This issue of maintaining the Petrodollar is actually many millions of times more important than whether Russia interferes with an election, North Korea tests an atomic bomb, there are humanitarian crises or human rights abuses somewhere in the world, or nearly any other issue you can possibly imagine. Therefore with its strong relationship with the CIA and military connections, unbeknownst to the public the ESF will execute its mandate and take any necessary steps to prevent the death of the Petrodollar. It will take any steps required to thwart the rejection of the US dollar in world trade, the rising of US dollar alternatives, and the abandonment of the US dollar as the global reserve currency.

Unfortunately, both history and current trends are going against the United States. For centuries, global reserve currencies typically maintained their status only about 80 to 110 years. In fact, before the US dollar won its position as the global reserve currency this status previously belonged to the monies of Britain, France, the Netherlands, Spain and Portugal each in turn.

The world's *reserve currency* is by definition the most popular currency in the world used for international trade. The nation which dominates global trade during a certain time period is usually the one whose money becomes the global reserve currency. Central banks then hold large quantities of that reserve currency in order to settle their global trade transactions, and thus all other currencies (and commodities) usually have values quoted in terms of their exchange rate to that currency.

If you are the one who issues the world's reserve currency then wealth travels into your country as you export your currency because you are exchanging paper you can just print up for *real goods and services* that come in. A fantastic opportunity for exchanging paper for real wealth becomes possible by which your country can become rich if it spends its money wisely to build itself up rather than just engage in conspicuous consumption. Dollars being exported from America have the capability of bringing wealth into the country if used wisely. If those dollars weren't needed for world trade anymore then they would be sold, hurting the dollar's value.

The US dollar's status as the world's reserve currency has already lasted as long as the reigns of Portugal and the Netherlands. Eventually a new reserve currency is coming that will not be the US dollar. This is inevitable. This is a fact. However, to preserve itself the U.S. must show resistance to change in order to prevent economic decline. It must make moves to block or counter anything that threatens its current status.

Let's review what would happen if nations abroad stopped using the US dollar as the global banking reserve currency, or simply stopped using the dollar in the majority of international trade. Foreign countries would begin sending the dollars back to the United States so that they could buy the new currency (or other vehicle) needed for exchange. They would also start dumping U.S. treasuries since they would no longer need them to hold the idle dollars they normally used for trade payment. The dollar simply wouldn't be the major component of banking reserves any longer. In short, the dollar along with Treasury bonds and bills would be dumped. The U.S. economy and financial system would be turned on their heads.

U.S. Treasuries and dollars would end up being be put on the market and sold. The Federal Reserve, with the inrush of dollars and Treasury bonds/bills that foreigners no longer wanted or needed, would be unable to print more dollars to pump up the American economy without a tremendous deteriorating effect.

The great benefit to the United States from everyone buying American T-bonds and T-bills (its debt) is that it can essentially borrow money from everyone else in its own currency. As the reserve currency that everyone accepts, the ability to print dollars is like owning a credit card with unlimited spending privileges. It allows you to create fiat credit-currency out of nothing and then use the free money to buy real assets in the world. The U.S. can buy things from overseas to power its economy just by printing more dollars ex nihilo and foreigners will happily accept them. Then those dollars will come back to buy American T-bonds, T-bills and other dollar-denominated assets ... all because the U.S. was able to create paper out of the air. If you work this right, you can finance all sorts of ventures and buy up all the productive assets and income streams in the world.

Due to being the world's reserve currency the U.S. can do things other countries simply cannot do, such as fund expensive wars just by printing paper. How valuable is that ability? The benefits of being able to just print up money that the world will blindly accept without objection or complaint is so great that the U.S. has, does, and will use all its military might to protect the dollar's status as the world's reserve currency.

With fewer dollar buyers, the U.S. would definitely lose its ability to simply print up money to pay for its sovereign debt, a privilege made possibly because other nations had always previously financed it. Now no one would want the dollar, and simply printing up new money or debt instruments would create dollar devaluation and hyperinflation within the country, just as happens with Third World nations who do this.

Dollar supremacy enables the U.S. to build military bases all over the world (or finance wars) by printing money accepted everywhere, meaning that the U.S. compels other nations to finance its wars. With this privilege extinguished, those military bases would be unaffordable real estate and have to close. In fact, the ability for the U.S. to wage war on its credit card would become absolutely curtailed. Some nations definitely want to see this happen.

The economic and financial devastation that would result within the United States, with a kill switch thus placed on its military operations worldwide, makes preservation of the US dollar as the reserve currency and primary global payments vehicle the #1 security issue we face as a nation. It is thousands of times more important than nearly any other issue you can think of.

Remember, as the world moves away from the US dollar it will stop buying Treasury bonds because nations will no longer need to park U.S. cash. Countries will sell off Treasury bonds in divestiture, diversifying into whatever is needed as the new trading vehicle they might require. The world will begin to settle trade using non-dollar payments so fewer dollars will be needed in circulation. As the dollar declines in popularity, many banks will falter due to less liquidity.

This will be like a shock to the U.S. economy that will also then face dramatically higher import prices. Half of the U.S. economy is based on imports, so if the dollar experiences a decrease in purchasing power (because it is rejected on the world stage) people will soon feel the daily agony of higher prices for many products. You may even have to do unthinkable things to get normal everyday commodities that disappear from the market.

Price inflation would become rampant if this happened. It would devastate the U.S. services-based economy that has lost its manufacturing sector. The domestic manufacturing and agricultural remainders might even respond by selling their products overseas for foreign currencies rather than internally for declining dollars. In time, severe consumer shortages would result not just due to higher priced imports but due to the fact that manufacturers (and farmers) would sell their best produce overseas, rather than at home, to obtain the more valuable foreign exchange.

The standing of the US dollar is therefore supported by the U.S. war machine to prevent this from ever happening. In recent years it has also been supported by QE for related reasons. The monetary policies of the Federal Reserve have massive influence worldwide, and the QE policies have both a domestic and international agenda.

QE uses hypermonetary inflation, at low interest rates, as a hidden Treasury bond purchase program because an increasing number of countries are buying fewer and fewer Treasury instruments. If the U.S. did not furtively use QE to buy rejected Treasury bonds then U.S. Treasury bond auctions would fail, bond prices would drop, interest rates would rise (making the U.S. debt even more unpayable), and the bonds would be rejected in even larger measure. Without QE the U.S. interest rates would increase dramatically and the national debt load would become unserviceable overnight.

At the same time these catastrophic financial outcomes are being prevented due to QE, the low interest rates engineered through quantitative easing are raising the cost structures for business rather than lowering them. This lowers business profitability and causes a retirement of capital because sufficient profits simply cannot be made at very low interest rates. In other words, QE still ends up destroying the economy, but in a different way.

The larger problem is that trying to maintain the dollar's dominance is fighting history and the law of impermanence. An inevitable change of status will occur, and the only question is when. Currently underway is a full frontal assault against the US dollar's dominant position as not only the global reserve currency but the international standard in trade. Together these two usages are what power the need for foreign countries to hold dollars in their banking systems, and that demand for the dollar is what keeps the value of the dollar high.

As more and more global trade is settled outside the US dollar, fewer Treasury bonds will be purchased by foreign nations who always use them to park their idle dollar cash. In fact, both US dollars and Treasury bonds or bills will be sold off through divesture to buy other currencies (the rising dominant players) or even gold. The U.S. will have to print tons of money to repurchase the T-bonds being dumped by foreign nations. The debasement of the money supply due to this printing will exacerbate the situation so that foreign holders of Treasury bonds will rush to sell even more, fueling a downward spiral. Treasury bonds will have to offer progressively higher yields along with a lower U.S. currency value in order to even attract any foreign buyers at all.

Since the U.S. is a massive importer, it must find a way to pay for the huge incoming supply of Treasury bonds that are even now being dumped by other nations. It cannot just printing money since this will lead to tremendous devaluation over time. Nonetheless, as the dollar's rejection on the world stage increases, eventually the U.S. will have to devalue its currency to maintain its international acceptance. This is one of the few things that can possibly slow down the foreign selling of Treasury bonds.

As previously stated, without a strong international demand for dollars, its value would plummet throwing the U.S. into a Third World condition. Therefore U.S. monetary authorities have turned a watchful eye towards the increase in world trade currently being conducted via the renminbi and other non-dollar payments, and have undertaken gold suppression schemes to keep the value of the dollar strong.

The fact that China is the world's largest importer of oil using renminbi, China is instituting direct currency swaps instead of using the US dollar, Russia is establishing a new gas-oil cartel accepting non-dollar payments, and Venezuela along with Iran are accepting non-dollar oil payments have all raised considerable concern.

Since the possible formation of any gold-backed currency, which involves internationally traded gold that carries no counterparty risk, also threatens the status of the dollar, the U.S. is also eyeing the gradual moves made by China to take control of the global gold pricing mechanism. The U.S. regularly suppresses the price of gold using those powers and worries that China would gain control of the mechanism.

People today frequently state that returning the world to the gold standard won't work as a means to handle currency adjustments and global trade are wrong because it did in the past. At the same time they object to the "gold standard" they don't recognize that the US dollar is actually based on an "oil standard." With the invention of the Petrodollar the value of the US dollar is actually implicitly backed by a commodity, only that commodity is oil rather than gold since you need the dollar to buy petroleum.

Without the Petrodollar standard the US dollar has no real asset backing whatsoever, which is what will put U.S. sovereign bonds at extreme risk upon the Petrodollar's collapse. Backing a currency with just tax revenues is actually just a game in fiat currency propaganda because that money can still become worthless. Consider, for future discussion, that if petroleum sales do not back the US dollar any longer then it may have to seek another asset as its foundation, and the only other logical backing alternative is gold, as it once was, although its price will have to rise substantially to make this feasible. This is another reason to become a long-term gold investor.

THE PETRODOLLAR

The Petrodollar standard actually began in the 1970s when Henry Kissinger and President Nixon struck a deal with Saudi Arabia that gave birth to the Petrodollar system. The terms of the deal were simple. The Saudis would only accept US dollars as the currency for their petroleum sales and would reinvest their surplus dollars from oil payments in U.S. Treasury instruments. The United States, in return, would sell arms to the Saudis and provide security guarantees for the nation. In short, the United States would both defend and sell military weapons to Saudi Arabia in return for all of its oil trade being denominated in US dollars.

With that agreement, the Saudis and all other Gulf nations started to sell their oil for dollar payments, and this has become the Petrodollar standard. The establishment of the Petrodollar was a way to create an ongoing demand for the dollar that was now unhinged from any gold backing. Forcing oil-exporting nations to keep their foreign currency reserves in US dollars basically created an ongoing demand for U.S. Treasury bonds, thus keeping U.S. interest rates and debt servicing costs low.

All major oil exporting nations now receive dollars for their petroleum and then turn around and park the incoming cash in U.S. Treasury bonds and bills. Since those nations wishing to buy oil must also acquire dollars, this buoying effect increases the demand for dollars in world financial markets. There is yet one more aspect to this matter to note. Many nations complain that the United States can virtually print up as much paper as it likes and thereby fund imperial ambitions. They want an end to America's rogue wars and invasions.

The Petrodollar standard has served for decades, but right now the standard is weakening. A major U.S. fear is that the OPEC countries begin to accept other currencies rather than just US dollars for oil payments, which would imperil the dollar's predominant status for world trade. The dollar's importance would surely decline with the loss of these money flows and it would probably cease to be the world's reserve currency. *Thus would then disappear all the advantages accruing to the United States from that status.* Even the ability to use the dollar as a method of bribery in geopolitics would deteriorate if its value declined. For all these reasons and many more, the U.S. insisted to Saudi Arabia that oil must be paid for in US dollars only.

This is the Petrodollar system that the U.S. has come to depend upon for its economy and *must defend* as the #1 strategic objective for the United States. When there are wars in the Mideast involving U.S. support they usually have nothing to do with oil supplies but with maintaining the U.S. Petrodollar system. The wars are largely, in one form or another, usually a way of making sure that countries continue to price oil in US dollar terms.

Fast forward to today. At present the U.S. faces the growing risk that if any of the major OPEC members dumps the US dollar for its petroleum sales then other members will quickly follow suit and the entire Petrodollar system collapses. This would leave the US dollar to be based on absolutely nothing tangible at all except for tax receipts and the "full faith and credit of the United States," which is simply not enough when U.S. debt levels have grown to exponential extremes.

If the Petrodollar system were to collapse then the U.S. economy could indeed collapse in turn. As explained, import prices would rise overnight and shortages would soon touch every sector of the economy. Unemployment would reach Great Depression levels and the dream that a "service-based economy" could exist would be exposed for the shameless sham that it is.

If the dollar began to collapse in value the resulting turmoil would financially and economically affect every nation on earth. Nations would scramble to exchange falling dollars for any other currency or asset (such as gold) of value. A collapse of the dollar would finally literally produce the biggest transfer of wealth in your lifetime.

This is why the U.S. fears Saudi Arabia accepting renminbi for its oil (or the Saudi kingdom falling since that would also imperil the Petrodollar), or Iran and Russia (or even Venezuela) trading their oil and gas for non-US dollar payments. If the trend catches hold, it will dramatically reduce the flow of dollars in world trade, and thus decrease the worldwide need for dollars. The Exchange Stabilization Fund, charged with protecting the value of the dollar, knows this.

IRAQ

Protecting the Petrodollar was therefore in fact the major reason why the U.S. went to war with Iraq back in 2003. This was actually due to the fact that Saddam Hussein was preparing to quit using the US dollar for his petroleum sales. Saddam Hussein had announced to the world that he was about to switch from pricing Iraq's oil exports from dollars to Euros. As newsworthy as this action was, it was sparsely reported in the corporate-controlled media.

When Saddam Hussein announced that Iraqi oil would be sold in Euros rather than dollars, sanctions and a U.S.-led invasion quickly followed. The United States, winning the conflict, quickly brought the sale of oil back to the US dollarfold.

Why the war? I agree with William Clark's *Petrodollar Warfare*, which was largely ignored by the mainstream media, that the intervention was to prevent Iraq from selling oil in currencies other than the dollar. The U.S. was desperate to prevent any OPEC oil transactions from converting to the Euro (or anything else) and needed to make an example of any nation who dared to threaten the existing Petrodollar system.

The U.S. routinely brands as a "terrorist" or "rogue state" any nation that wishes to supplant the US dollar with a new currency or precious metals alternative. That nation is immediately labeled a hostile adversary in some way that then allows it to illegally attack that nation. For instance, the American government might state that it wishes to "liberate" a people from a brutal regime or that the country has "weapons of mass destruction" (most every nation does, including the U.S.) when they are only clever guises to mask its true intent, which is to preserve the full integrity of the Petrodollar system. The U.S. will take all sorts of extreme measures, including even war (and certainly assassinations), to prevent any first steps that might threaten the Petrodollar's collapse.

Petropolitics are all about maintaining the US dollar as the single payments vehicle for the global oil trade. The Iraqi invasion was not about oil because global oil supply was never threatened, and it is always simply cheaper to buy petroleum on the market than invade a country. Its availability was never an issue at stake. So yes, the U.S. has indeed gone to war at least once to protect the Petrodollar. If an oil producing nation wants to switch away from the dollar for its petroleum sales, the message being broadcast is that *you will be targeted so don't do this.*

The real reason the U.S. now focuses on Iran as its latest enemy is also because Iran also wishes to dump the Petrodollar too. In fact, Iran is already selling its oil for currencies other than the dollar, which makes Iran a clear enemy. The problem with invading Iran, however, is that it is a country with exceptional military strength, with a long history and around 80 million inhabitants. It is also supported by China and Russia. Therefore the U.S. has to maneuver in other ways in order to be able to make the strike it wants. The whole Arab world might be besieged.

LIBYA

The former U.S. intervention in Libya that killed Colonel Muammar Gaddafi was also about opposing a currency plan to replace the US dollar for oil sales. In this case, Libya was Africa's largest oil producer. Gaddafi had not only modernized his nation, turning it into the showpiece of Africa, but also created a Pan-African plan to introduce the gold dinar, a single currency based in gold, to African petroleum nations and Middle eastern nations to replace the dollar in world oil trade. This plan certainly carried the potential to bring down the US dollar.

At the World Motaba Conference organized by Libya, Gaddafi called on African and Muslim nations to pull together to create this new gold dinar currency to rival the dollar and Euro. The proposal was that they should sell their oil only for the new gold dinar. This would effectively reprice oil in gold, bypassing the US dollar entirely.

To the U.S. this was an incredible threat that would shift the economic balance of the world. Not only would the dollar be displaced and deposed, but the alternative was a more honest gold-backed currency instead of the oil-backed Petrodollar. Gold was an international asset without counterparty risks whose price would be difficult to manipulate, so the threat to the dollar's dominance was extreme.

The U.S. couldn't afford to let anything happen, such as a rise in the price of oil in gold or abandonment of the dollar in the oil trade. While these moves would strengthen all of Africa since they would lead to currencies being based on sound money, the move certainly was not welcomed by the monetary elites who run the western central banks. They no doubt wanted this threat terminated, which entailed Gaddafi's immediate dismissal so that he could never raise the plan again.

Just a short time after announcing these plans a Libyan rebellion suddenly arose backed by NATO forces. In the early weeks of the conflict the rebels even broadcast their creation of a new national oil company and the replacement of Libya's state-owned central bank. What rebel group in history creates a new central bank in the midst of a civil war with the opponent still in power? Isn't that something you normally do *after* you triumph over an entrenched political power?

The rebels out of nowhere somehow had enough time,

foresight and expertise to establish a new Central Bank of Libya in Benghazi and form a new national oil company without any external guidance. Wow, those forward-thinking rebels must have thought that central banking was really important!

One popular blog called *The Economic Collapse* aptly commented, "What a skilled bunch of rebels — they can fight a war during the day and draw up a new central bank and a new national oil company at night without any outside help whatsoever. If only the rest of us were so versatile! ... Apparently someone felt that it was very important to get pesky matters such as control of the banks and control of the money supply out of the way even before a new government is formed."

Gaddafi himself was killed in the fighting. His gold dinar plan went with him to the grave while his nation's 150 tons of gold also somehow disappeared into London vaults. As to its new central bank, observers noted that Libya's old central bank was one of the few left in the world that was entirely state-owned, meaning that the Libyan government created its own money and thus avoided unmanageable levels of national debt. In printing its own money Libya was out of the control reach of foreign powers who then had no power-brokering dominion or leverage over the country. The new Libyan bank, however, has joined the standard monetary practices of the league of compliant nations.

QATAR

The small Arab country of Qatar, a leading liquid natural gas producer located on the waistline of Saudi Arabia, is currently suffering troubles as yet another example of Petrodollar concerns in play. Qatar had wanted to build a natural gas pipeline to supply its European clients, but the pipeline had to travel through Syria. The source of the gas is one of the largest natural gas fields on earth, located beneath the Persian Gulf (North Dome or South Pars field) in an area jointly owned by Qatar and Iran.

In an incredibly complicated story, the U.S. supported the Qatari pipeline since Qatar would sell its natural gas in dollars. However, Iran and Russia also wanted a Syrian pipeline with the intent to sell Iranian gas in non-dollar currencies. Thus we had the Syrian War, which was actually due to gas pipelines and the U.S. wanting to secure dollar payments for that gas. This is why the United States military was used to help wage the Syrian War. It had nothing to do with anything other than the fact that Syria was allowing a non-dollar payments gas pipeline through its territory. The United States had to defeat this.

Qatar finally threw in the towel of opposition against Syria when it appeared that Russia won the fighting against the U.S. supported forces. The Iranian-Russian gas pipeline had won, so Qatar logically switched sides out of self-interest. Basically, with the U.S. losing and the Russians winning Qatar decided to reach a deal with Iran to export liquefied natural gas from their jointly held massive gas field.

So Qatar has recently changed sides. It originally supported the Saudi-Iraqi pipeline to supply Europe but now supports the Iranian-Russian pipeline to supply Europe, to be paid in non-dollar terms. The core of the non-Gulf region will therefore now subscribe to the Iranian-Russian gas pipeline through Syria. If the OPEC Petrodollar standard ever becomes void, this Iranian-Russian gas line will grow into an even bigger consortium to fill the void with a new cartel that accepts payments in non-dollar terms.

This type of development might actually form the backbone for the newly arising Eurasian trade zone. The U.S. is justifiably worried in the extreme, so both Russia and Iran have become its predominant enemies, with China in the wings. Unfortunately for the U.S., it cannot take on any of these countries singly or in combination. Therefore I believe that the fate of the Petrodollar is sealed it will die.

The U.S. always acts to discourage nations from exiting the dollar universe, and most of its Mideast conflicts have been based on manipulative variations of this main agenda. Israel and Saudi Arabia are aligned to this concern due to their own interests, which constitute entirely different agendas such as the fear of Iran. Israel and Saudi Arabia also share a common interest involving the greater Arab Muslim world, which is to keep these countries in a state of chaos, disunity and weakness so that they can more easily be dominated and controlled.

The U.S. has been putting pressure on Qatar to still support the non-Iranian plan. However, Qatar holds some strong trump cards so as to be able to do its own bidding and determine its own future. It not only has rights to the natural gas field in question but hosts the largest US military base in the Mideast. It also has Turkish soldiers within its border, and a strong region-wide propaganda network. Its news organization, Al Jazeera, rankles Mideastern nations and the U.S. because it focuses on actual news and covers truth rather than local propaganda. It is a tremendous asset of the nation that the surrounding regions fear.

In the final analysis, Washington is not going to let go of its largest military base in the Mideast, or cede it to Saudi Arabia, by going against Qatar. The outcome will likely be a stalemate.

The recent push against Qatar by other Arab nations, who are all equally guilty of funding terrorism although they accuse Qatar of this deed, is just further evidence that the Petrodollar foundation is weakening and needs to be braced. The entire problem is based on the dollar losing a degree of trade status, so it will get delicate since Qatar cannot be invaded.

CHINA AND RUSSIA

While China hasn't been attacked in any of these frays, China has been making extensive moves to stop using the US dollar in its bilateral trade, has started dumping its extensive U.S. Treasury bond holdings, created alternative payment routes that bypass US dollar control, created international banking institutions (Asian Infrastructure Investment Bank and BRICS Development Bank) that wrench control from a U.S. dominated financial world (the World Bank, IMF, etc.), and has even made initial efforts to gain control of the physical gold market.

In other words, China is making slow and careful moves to bypass any reliance on the US dollar, creating great economic institutions to advance its interests (like the U.S. did following WWII) and has even been purchasing gold in order to protect itself should the dollar (and thus Treasury bonds) go bust, which would cause the value of precious metals to skyrocket. China is even maneuvering so that the world oil market will switch out of the dollar payments mechanism (the Petrodollar) into gold and other currencies, thus de-dollarizing the world's dependence on U.S. currency as its main trade payments vehicle.

Being a large trading partner and Treasury bond holder whom the United States cannot win against in a war, the U.S. has few means to bully China into ceasing its de-dollarization trend. However, the U.S. is probing for weakness and threatening China with trade sanctions to thwart its efforts and gain leverage against it.

Russia has also been making similar de-dollarization moves as China at the same time. Russia was the first country to agree to accept renminbi for its oil. Seeing Russia as possibly a weaker power it might be able to topple or coerce the U.S. power elite have been focusing on turning Russia into an enemy with all sorts of sanctions and other claims to thwart its growing importance. Unfortunately for the U.S., Russia has already priced its oil in non-dollar terms and has very little foreign debt that can be leveraged against it. All the coordinated U.S. moves against Russia have provoked responses that have actually strengthened rather than weakened the nation.

The U.S. cannot go against both the Russian and Chinese nations at the same time, so it is attempting to weaken one after the other. Only if the U.S. actually topples Russia, which it cannot do (since Russia is stronger militarily and would also receive support from China and Iran), can it thwart the de-dollarization trends of Russia and China together. That not being possible, the U.S. has no choice but to surrender to the forward march of the renminbi and eventual dollar replacement. Gold and silver will most probably rear their heads as part of the on-going de-dollarization movement. Many nations will probably choose to eventually buy the precious metals over the US dollar because even now they are looking to distance themselves from the influence of the Federal Reserve along with America's unchecked influences in undeclared wars and catastrophic foreign policies.

The ESF is charged with defending the US dollar in this precarious situation, which is compounded by the extremely high U.S. debt levels and a weak economy hollowed out due to the loss of America's manufacturing base. Internationally the ESF usually defends the dollar through currency interventions, but unconventionally it has been known to fund covert operations for its objectives. Who knows what it is doing at present?

Domestically, the ESF and Federal Reserve have been teaming up and intervening in various ways to prop up the US dollar even though many nations are shedding their U.S. Treasury bonds at this time and switching to non-dollar alternatives. The U.S. has definitely recruited the Federal Reserve's resources to prop up the dollar, and as you can see from history, is even willing to go to war to protect its value. With the major de-dollarization trends afoot, the dollar's preeminence will not stand much longer.

4
THE RISE OF BANKISM

Here are the economic and financial situations that, for whatever reasons they have occurred, the U.S. finds itself in at present, and what a predicament it is. The economic situation first.

Over the past two decades the U.S. outsourced its manufacturing base to developing nations with lower labor costs, and U.S. jobs disappeared overseas with this trend. This not only eviscerated the domestic U.S. manufacturing base, decreasing U.S. exports and increasing America's trade imbalance, but absolutely gutted the middle class who saw their jobs go offshore. American labor increasingly took on a Third World appearance as the high value added jobs that typically powered the middle class disappeared. The U.S. government, permitting and even encouraging labor's movement overseas along with its replacement through foreign worker visas, actually became the saboteur of American labor!

With manufacturing in domestic decline all sorts of other jobs followed in being shuttled offshore to lower cost nations. Eventually even the customer service and marketing jobs left America when the language skills, internet connections and telecommunications permitted it.

Thus the American economy was slowly gutted like a dead fish, and now students graduating from college cannot easily find jobs but commonly live in their parents' basements. If 25-year olds rack up unpayable student loans and cannot afford to form households then what will support housing prices in the future and the market for items like home furnishings? If full-time jobs are destroyed and replaced with part-time jobs then from where will come the money for the consumer spending that normally powers the U.S. economy?

With the disappearance of working and middle class jobs went the underpinnings of America's consumer demand economy. The American economy is based upon consumer debt, which is now a tremendous problem because consumers are already at the upper reaches of their debt limits. Consumers are already at "peak debt" with no more debt/loans they can handle to stimulate more spending.

To have based the economy upon consumer debt is a stupid idea in the first place. To think that a strong economy can be created solely upon the foundation of financial services and financial engineering as an economic core is a delusion too. You cannot have a healthy, strong long-lasting economy based on debt and consumerism. You cannot have a strong economy that avoids the business investment road of wealth production, and expect it to provide an endless way of life that produces stable household incomes via stimulated consumption. You cannot create a healthy economy through financial paper shenanigans.

These false notions all originated with Wall Street bankers and its intellectual elites looking for an alternative to replace our lost manufacturing sector with a new economic core. Wall Street banking, and its desire for debt-based money flows derived from capturing consumers completely, has provided the intellectual guidance to all this nonsense including the government's emphasis on Bankism as a solution.

This unhealthy thinking has posited Bankism as a replacement for manufacturing. It postulates that the real economic investment that previously built America and made it strong can be replaced by an emphasis on the financial sector, debt stimulus and the financialization or commodification of debt. It believes that a vibrant, healthy economy can be based primarily on the financial sector of loans, insurance, and real estate rather than the production of real goods and services.

We are now seeing the inevitable climax that was always fated to occur in a consumption-based economy stimulated by debt where manufacturing disappears. With labor already at "peak debt" and in danger of job losses or less remunerative jobs, national consumer demand is now stifled. Stimulus is necessary to keep the economy afloat even though consumers are also at their debt limit with "peak things," so stimulus doesn't work as well anymore. We are near the end of the biggest credit bubble in history that was used to stimulate the economy when production left home shores, and now that bubble is due to pop. The results in America will be economically devastating.

Right now consumers lacking well-paying jobs can no longer expand their spending with more credit, so new investment no longer appeals to smart businesses (who for various reasons aren't getting ready access to bank loans). A decrease in the demand for goods and services has destroyed the normally expected investment opportunities for large firms *and* small entrepreneurs who are the very people who usually create jobs in the American economy.

The Fed has compounded matters by making debt dirt cheap (as a stimulus), but the banks have put this nearly free money into the financial engineering of trading games instead of making loans to the productive Main Street segments of the economy. Asset prices, particularly stocks and real estate, have risen due to financial engineering games and bankers leveraging their "free money" to buy assets. However, there is no increasing prosperity in the real economy nor is any real economic growth to be seen.

The rise in paper asset prices has somewhat cushioned the negative impact being felt by pension funds and insurance companies who are struggling because they need higher interest rates to keep afloat. It has also helped insolvent banks that require substantial non-lending profits to avoid an impending bankruptcy. In short, the central banking activity of the Fed has diverted funds to speculative activity rather than real productivity in the economy, and the Fed did this simply for its buoying effect. The government, though its unwise monetary policies, has seen to the gutting of the country's manufacturing base so it has turned to Bankism hoping to provide a replacement stimulus. This cannot last forever.

Despite low interest debt pumping by the Fed, the American economy still hasn't been able to go anywhere and businesses have been substituting part-time jobs for full-time jobs. The cost burdens of Obamacare have served as an extra job killer that has additionally shuttled many full-time jobs into part-time positions.

Without well-paying jobs there hasn't been adequate incomes to support the taxable base of states and local governments, so they have started running into fiscal problems, especially with pensions coming due that are not being funded by higher interest rates either. No factories equals no jobs, equals no consumer demand, equals no taxable incomes, equals no city and state revenues. The offshoring of jobs has destroyed the U.S. labor movement and gutted the real economy.

Because American manufactures fewer things that it can now sell to foreigners since those very items are now being produced by factories abroad (and even the taxable earnings of those U.S. foreign-held factories were not being returned to America), the government has had to turn to new ways to stimulate the economy. Thus the boom and bust cycle of asset pumping was born in order to replace the lost base of prosperity with temporary short-term swings.

Of all the financial options available, debt has become the only remaining possible stimulus for the economy but it has been having less and less impact on real growth. The debt has also turned us from a productive economy into an extractive economy that drains producers. As stated, the U.S. turned to Bankism and the road of financialization as a replacement for manufacturing, and has tried valiantly to substitute the expansion of interest, leverage and speculation (as well as an intensified concentration on finance, insurance and real estate) for the real expansion of goods and services. The financial sector profits from synthetic transactions that have nothing to do with the real production of goods and services in the economy. The smartest people know that the quickest way to make millions now is not by slowly building a real business, but by working on some investment banking deal or creating a vein of wealth based on commoditized assets, credit and leverage. This trend cannot last long.

"Financialization," a "services-based economy" or even a "financial sector-based economy" all sound like they might be viable roads to prosperity, but of course they are not. Interest bearing debt grows exponentially in an economy while the productive economy grows only in an S-curve, meaning that with a financialization emphasis the economy will create debt faster than its ability to repay. This always causes economic breakdowns. During the course of its long development, U.S. industry replaced agriculture as the primary economic base of American society, but finance and financialization cannot in turn replace manufacturing. Even so, the U.S. government turned the country into a casino economy by substituting the issuance and trading of debt and monetary manipulation for a solid economy that makes real things.

FINANCIALIZATION AND BANKISM RISE

This is how and why banking and finance replaced manufacturing as the center of the American economy. A nation's wealth is based on its ability to produce valuable goods, and yet that ability was destroyed in America. With the death of domestic manufacturing because of countless corporations offshoring for higher profits, the U.S. government turned to the financial sector, financialization and financial engineering to power the domestic growth engine. It turned to bankers making loans in order to create boom cycles of temporary stimulus, followed by predictable busts. The financialization of loans for home mortgages, car purchases and college tuitions funneled tremendous economic rewards to banks making use of cheap credit and excessive leverage. With financialization the big money wasn't made on the loans but on processing, packaging and marketing them globally. Unfortunately, all the western economies taking this route have been financialized in a predatory way that sacrifices the public interest to the interests of the financial sector, which is another problem with Bankism once again.

The big problem with financialization as a stimulus is that it both kills capital and requires ever larger and more extreme policies to keep it going unless the rot of bad debt it creates is cleared to the very core. An economy with a rising dependence on debt and leverage needs to employ them at an increasing rate just to keep things steady at the status quo or at a low rate of growth. Therefore the only way to keep the economic engines running when you depend on increasing debt levels, which in themselves end up destroying businesses, is by dissolving another barrier of financial discipline. At each new step of leverage you have to make worse loans to get any sort of propping effect. As the cracks in the dam get bigger, the actions you need to take must become more dramatic.

In other words, financialization requires exponential growth to remain a support mechanism while at the same time its penetration progressively hollows out the real economy. Furthermore, you also progressively get less for more as financialization grows in quantity. This is neither sustainable nor sound finance. The steps you must take to keep things at just status quo might at first seem inconsequential but the consequences soon pile up due to massive changes beneath the surface. Eventually, insufficient wealth is generated to pay the interest on the debt already undertaken, so you end up only being able to pay it via a Ponzi scheme that issues more debt at a lower cost to pay for the old. The leveraging up employs less and less base collateral so what you eventually get, which is our precarious situation now, is a veritable house of cards.

When did this financialization trend as a proposed solution for problems first start to appear in the U.S.? There is no one date that pinpoints the first beginnings, but a good start is when the United States went off the gold standard in 1971. Instead of settling trade accounts in gold you then had to settle them in US dollars. Ever since that time, *Money, Markets and Sovereignty* (by Benn Steil and Manuel Hinds) reminds us that the only period in which humanity has not based its currency in gold has been the last five decades. On the other hand, when the dollar's value was linked to gold from 1789 to 1971 the U.S. was the most successful of any major country!

In the 1980s the U.S. monetary authorities then started loosening restrictions on bank leveraging. Leveraging eventually went up to 33:1 in some firms, meaning that a loss of just 3% in mortgage portfolios would produce bank insolvency. This degree of leveraging created incredible levels of systemic risk and played a great role in what was to follow.

Next, in 1999 Congress also got rid of the Glass-Steagall Act, which had wisely separated commercial banking from investment banking for years. With these restrictions gone, the banks were now able to openly pursue speculation for profits by trading stocks and bonds on Wall Street instead of being dependent on making loans to Main Street. Banks started speculating with *your money*, leveraging themselves in trading and financial games by using money that wasn't theirs. By dismantling the previous regulatory framework the government encouraged an anything-goes environment that in time eventually produced the Great Recession of 2008-2009.

After getting rid of Glass-Steagall, the government also loosened consumer lending standards so that nearly anyone who applied could get a mortgage with a "liar loan" by simply stating their income, true or false. The initial beginnings of the liar loans can definitively be traced back to 1988 when a bank called Guardian Savings and Loan issued the first "subprime" mortgage bond. It did this by packaging together all the mortgages it had made to borrowers with bad credit and then sold the bond to other banks and investors. Pretty soon all the banks were doing this.

Seeing this as a way to pump up the economy since the manufacturing sector was being exported, the monetary authorities took an anti-regulatory stance to these loans, which then put Bankism into high gear. They effectively looked the other way in order to produce a short-term economic bump as the banks made aggressive loans to high-risk borrowers with bad credit, which they would compile and then sell in syndicated packages.

Since the originating banks weren't keeping the loans on their books, they didn't have to worry about declining credit standards themselves. Thus they busily originated loans to bad borrowers at full steam in order to pocket the fees, and were offloading the risks onto the new loan owners through syndication. Banks were lending to everyone they could regardless of people's capacity to pay back since the banks wouldn't suffer any losses at all. They simply passed the risks onto another investor. In this way the risks spread to the entire global financial system.

From the initial steps of mortgage securitization arose non-bank mortgage originators and the sub-prime mortgage industry. Then came J.P. Morgan's invention of the CDO, or collateralized debt obligation. All sorts of other financial innovations abounded, each termed "safe enough for institutional investors." Seeking profits, the ratings agencies put their seal of approval on these new instruments to experience their most profitable years in history.

As noted, along the way the Greenspan Fed and Clinton administration turned a blind eye to all the lending excesses and abuses involved with these new vehicles. The government, in need, had an anti-regulatory bias because of the pumping stimulus this was producing for the lagging economy gutted by factory and job migrations overseas.

Given the excessive monetary easing that the Fed engineered at the same time as all these loans, the Fed helped create a credit boom that found its way - via financial innovation, lax governance (both private and public), and misaligned incentives - into excessively buoying the housing market. Housing prices shot up with all the cheap money available to buyers who actually weren't qualified for mortgages, liar loans or otherwise, but who were given mortgages anyway.

Remember that pension funds, insurance companies and mutual funds are always seeking high yields for their portfolios, but during all this time the Fed was lowering rates to fuel the boom. Those lower interest rates in turn encouraged investors seeking higher yields to take on riskier investments than they otherwise would have. With interest rates declining due to the Fed's monetary interventions, yield-seeking institutions had no other high yielding alternatives available that might generate the incomes they needed. Thus they put the higher yielding toxic mortgage bonds, which were being created out of this mess, into their portfolios. Wall Street pushed these sales, calling everything "safe," because it wanted the fees.

The net result of all this was that the balance sheets of financial institutions swelled with toxic loans, making those portfolios exceptionally vulnerable to decline. The United States even started exporting its problem because Freddie Mac and Fannie Mae mortgages were being sold all over the world; the dirty money game went global. At the same time, the new financial games made participating banks become so large that they had to be protected since their collapse was now deemed a threat to the economy.

"Too Big To Fail" became the de facto government Bankism policy of supporting the banks, no matter how shaky their finances or activities, to keep the spin machine going. Bankers and financial executives who performed criminal deeds to facilitate the mess also became "Too Big To Jail" in order to show implicit government support of the only machinery holding up the economy.

There is no more effective deterrent for crime than jail. The federal regulators, however, let the big banks and their highly paid executives off the hook when they broke the law thus ending personal accountability. Bankism was on!

The political power of the large banks and supposed "risks of economic impacts" from major prosecutions effectively insulated executives from criminal charges for crimes that should have been pursued. Not a single major banker went to jail for crimes committed during the subprime mortgage scandal – the great financial meltdown of 2008-2009 – that cost millions of Americans their jobs and homes and destroyed finances worldwide. Under current legal and regulatory arrangements the boards and financial executives faced no liability for the harm they caused.

In this era of Bankism gone haywire, U.S. financial regulators definitely turned a blind eye to regulating and the government threw away any attempts to criminally prosecute law-breaking financiers. It simply charged the banks fees and penalties for their misdoings, which became merely a cost of doing business. For instance, Wachovia bank paid a mere $160 million fee for running a $420 billion Mexican narco money laundering operation. It then simply wrote off this fee as a cost of doing business.

According to Reuters, there are four major billion dollar legal settlements with financial institutions since 2012 including JPMorgan Chase ($13 billion), Bank of America ($16.6 billion), Citibank ($7 billion) and Morgan Stanley ($3.2 billion). As an example, in 2013 JPMorgan Chase agreed to pay a $13 billion settlement to the U.S. government (the largest ever with a single institution in US history) related to the sale of bad mortgages to government-sponsored Fannie Mae and Freddie Mac. To JPMorgan Chase this too must have just seemed like a cost of business because its board of directors awarded CEO Jamie Dimon a 74% pay increase that same year.

If we truly wish to reform the excesses in the banking system that put our general economy and the public welfare at risk, we must temper Bankism by convicting and imprisoning bankers who commit fraud. We must stop granting wavers to the consequences called for by law, and prohibit corporations from taking tax deductions for fines.

Returning to history, the banks themselves and other financial institutions were investing boatloads in the packaged mortgage instruments for their high yields, and then the inevitable happened. Eventually lenders started defaulting on the loans they couldn't afford that should never have been granted, and thus started the Great Recession of 2008-2009. The value of toxic subprime loans started going underwater, meaning that borrowers owed more on their mortgages than their homes were worth. The markets crashed and the value of these loans fell dramatically. There were countless job losses, foreclosures, bankruptcies and write-offs in America. As homeowners began defaulting on mortgages, investment portfolios that bought these toxic assets collapsed, bringing much of the U.S. economy and the nation's largest banks into near default. To say that the Great Recession was a mess is a gross understatement.

Since the banks were now loaded with toxic debt that wouldn't ever be repaid, their balance sheets spelled insolvency. Therefore honest mark-to-market accounting was removed from marketplace regulation since firms were effectively bankrupt but needed some way to hide the fact. In a state of emergency, the government and the Federal Reserve now had to find some way to quickly supply liquidity to insolvent Wall Street banks to prevent their actual bankruptcy. However, they had to do this without tipping everyone off to the severity of the problem so as to avoid panic. This is why QE was invented.

Here's the dilemma that the Fed now faced. If financial firms were forced to declare the real value of their toxic mortgage securities then most of them would certainly face bankruptcy, including the largest banks in the nation (shareholders of the Fed). This true state of affairs had to be hidden to allow the dead banks to continue operating without pulling the plug. Though technically broken, through various means they were given leeway in hopes they would become profitable enough over time to cover their losses and revitalize. This gave rise to the term "zombie bank" to describe institutions that were like the walking dead – technically bankrupt but still functioning. Debts that cannot be paid won't be paid so what else was the government to do other than delay a reckoning?

Bankism had taken hold. The big banks and financial institutions originating and investing in bad loans had become so central to the economy that they had become untouchable. They had to be saved in any way possible. The Fed, whose shareholders are the big banks themselves, didn't want the big banks to be declared bankrupt, broken up and recapitalized so they made sure this didn't happen. Paradoxically, after all the smoke eventually cleared the big banks, although financially insolvent in most respects, ended up becoming just that much more dominant.

In the meantime, knowing that a system-wide bail-out was necessary the U.S. monetary authorities had to come up with a plan. They decided to buy all the bad debt owned by the banks by issuing dollars, and disguised the plan by calling it a "stimulus," namely quantitative easing or QE. They decided to buy as much bad debt as possible and stash it away at public expense on the Fed's balance sheet. The Fed simply bought it up and put it on its own books by printing money and exchanging it for the toxic mortgages. The Fed and Treasury acted in an obliging way that first and foremost protected the banks and creditors rather than the Main Street public! This was Bankism at its best.

The great 2008 Bailout followed the rules of Bankism because it saved the banks from bankruptcy, but didn't save the American economy even though the Fed purchased the toxic debt of banks to hide the problems on its books. The net result of the bailout efforts basically transferred wealth and income to the financial sector, which should have been financially punished for its excesses, while at the same time the effects of the bailout impoverished America's middle class.

Truckloads of money were effectively given to the banks to erase their bad investments, but because the banks had stopped lending this "easy money" never made it to Main Street businesses that normally create jobs for the working class. The easy money from the Fed, printed out of thin air, made it to the banks to keep them afloat but never made it to the middle class to help the national economy. It stayed in the coffers of banks needing bailouts to cover their bad loans and investments, and some was even used to pay bank dividends or repurchase stock shares. Thus the Federal Reserve demonstrated its primary hidden mandate, *which is to always help its shareholder bankers rather than the public*. This is Bankism at its core.

The Fed's easy money policy of quantitative easing essentially entailed creating money out of thin air to buy toxic mortgage debt and remove that bad debt from bank balance sheets. The Fed turned to the hypermonetary inflation of QE to keep the big banks liquid. This also required elaborate derivative schemes (highly leveraged interest rate swap derivatives), mostly kept secret, involving pumped up artificial demand for Treasury bonds to help manage the low interest rates that were keeping the Too Big To Fail banks solvent.

The Fed had to keep domestic interest rates low in order to finance the Treasury debt it was issuing to buy up the toxic debt it was trying to retire. If it increased the interest rates this would just make its job harder by putting an even bigger hamper on the economy and economic growth. Through the QE program the Fed ended up purchasing both toxic mortgage backed securities *and* U.S. government debt using newly minted money.

The first round of quantitative easing pushed down short-term interest rates by purchasing Treasury bills. Later versions of QE purchased Treasury bonds to push down long-term Treasury rates, which lowered yields. The lower interest rates not only reduced the burden of servicing all the debt being created, but were also necessary to give large banks the ability to borrow and speculate using leverage to possibly cover some of their losses.

QE decreased the borrowing cost of banks that were starved for profits, and so they made ample use of leverage and started purchasing equities for returns while corporations used the low rates to buy back their stocks, thus fueling a crazy stock market equities boom instead of a housing boom. Financialization, which expands debt, leverage and speculation in an economy, had once again become the means to temporarily prop up the economy, but the apparent prosperity was a house of cards.

The entire QE process brought the Fed funds rate to nearly zero, whereupon it became known as the zero interest rate policy or ZIRP. With the exponentially growing need of more and more economic stimulus over time, the government had backed itself into a corner and now needed a zero interest rate policy to keep the bad banks and the whole system of debt afloat. In order to survive all the debt it had issued and keep any possible stimulus working, the government engineered interest rates to hover near the lowest levels they have ever been in 5,000 years of recorded history! Central banks in some nations even moved their rates to below zero – a negative interest rate policy (NIRP) whose very existence indicated a massive failure in the global financial system - and they initiated even larger scale asset purchases in order to monetize their official debts.

Unfortunately, extremely low interest rates now failed to stimulate more new mortgages or lending. Therefore the debt arena was switched. Instead of mortgage or business loans the same game of loan explosions started to be played in student college loans as well as in subprime car loans to stimulate the economy. As anyone could easily predict, both markets are now in danger of massive defaults, and will eventually have to receive public bailouts to protect the banks again.

This boom-bust cycle as a form of stimulus just doesn't produce prosperity. In fact, the trouble with asset bubbles as a form of stimulus is that you have to keep inflating them or they deflate when the music stops. They will also eventually explode if you keep inflating them to super-nova status. Inflate it too much and a balloon always pops.

In the case of car loans and student loans, once again the authorities have chosen finance and financial engineering rather than manufacturing as an economic stimulus, which had formerly served the nation for decades. Shooting itself in the foot so that it is permanently crippled and always looking for bandages, the U.S. did itself in when it unwisely allowed real production to be exported from the economy so that corporations could make more profits. How can the U.S. sustain itself if it doesn't produce anything of real value anymore?

Bankism has now become one of the dominant mechanisms that powers the U.S. economy. With this switch from Main Street and manufacturing jobs to financial stimulus games, which create fiat paper out of thin air or use financial engineering to manipulate markets, the U.S. has hit two birds with one stone and actually eroded both its banking system *and* real economy. The problem for Americans is that the government regards the needs of the American people as an obstacle to the profits of Wall Street and the megabanks that dominate Bankism. Finance is not a productive activity so the path of Bankism that the government has chosen has actually produced a grave existential threat to the nation.

In short, the chronically loose monetary policy did little to help the Main Street economy, but did everything to help Wall Street. The standard economic stimulus cycle is now as follows. Virtually free money is now regularly supplied to financial institutions, released from former regulatory shackles that protected the public, to boom fund aggressively leveraged speculation that buoys Wall Street. This financial speculation, using nearly free money applied with leverage, drives the prices of stocks and other paper assets dramatically higher (booms) to unrealistic, unsustainable levels that will inevitably collapse in crashes (busts). The Fed will then start the process all over again by re-inflating the markets with fresh liquidity infusions.

Wall Street is no longer supporting Main Street but simply focused on the banks of Wall Street. It took a long time, but finance, real estate and insurance have been selected to replace industrial capitalism as the heart of the American economy. Financial games, lead by the Wall Street banks, have become the new norm for the economy. With Bankism, the financial institutions have become the dominant concern of the monetary authorities rather than the aggregate health of the national economy in total.

The real U.S. economy has become weak because of

this rampant road of financialism. It is now unable to repay its debt load, and hidden insolvency threatens both America and the entire world economy through the domino effect. The trick is to hide this fact in order to keep the rollercoaster going as long as possible, hence no official dares to publicly say that U.S. finances are now characteristic of a Third World nation, but they are.

Each one of these steps of deterioration was huge. At every point along the way the U.S. monetary authorities had to keep going to further extremes to keep the system from imploding. For instance, both Alan Greenspan and Ben Bernanke poured liquidity onto every small crisis so that the debt engine kept growing. As explained, the banking system kept issuing such an incredible amount of toxic debt that it eventually became the Great Recession that nearly destroyed the nation. The Fed had to step in and buy up all this debt, issuing new debt in its place. The Federal Reserve balance sheet now holds trillions of this bad debt of toxic assets it removed from the banking system in an attempt to preserve its integrity. Bankism means that the public must pay for all this mess, not the banks. The government isn't even requiring the most offensive banks to be reorganized.

Of course the whole system is an unsustainable house of cards without any real backing anymore, but no one dares to say anything near to the truth for fear the bubble will pop should the truth be revealed. Loan demand is now down, so the stimulating effects of new debt have also diminished. Few in the economy now qualify for new loans or want to borrow money even at low interest rates anyway. The banks and government also cannot force private lending onto people in order to create any new asset bubbles so there is very little ammo left from increasing the debt stimulus.

In short, the U.S. turned to debt and credit as a way to replace manufacturing. It created all sorts of conditions ripe for the granting of incredible amounts of shaky credit, and then institutionalized it in packaged vehicles that it sold to American banks and the rest of the world. The U.S. thereby exported a bad credit problem everywhere and put the whole world at risk. By selling the packaged loans overseas the U.S. banks created a worldwide problem of toxic debt load that has imperiled the financial systems of countless nations across the globe. These activities have actually threatened the entire global financial system, which has had to turn to ZIRP and then NIRP in order to keep everything together. No one can now get out of these policies.

In order to keep things together in America the Fed has only needed a low to zero interest rate policy so far. It has also pursued a low interest rate policy based on the assumption that low interest rates stimulate economic growth by boosting investment and consumption. However, this assumption no longer holds true in today's world. More debt is not helping anymore. Furthermore, we cannot even grow ourselves out of the debt we already have, whose total is now a gigantic burden. A default will have to ensue.

Compounding matters even moreso is that fact that the debt bubble is now so large that raising interest rates would pop it by causing defaults – thus we will probably have ZIRP and NIRP nearly forever in the world unless the deck is cleared of the toxic debt in its entirety. As stated previously, the very existence of NIRP (negative interest rates), where you actually lose money by depositing it with the government, shows that world financial systems are truly broken. At present the U.S. system itself must be artificially held together by massive derivative machinery, which logic tells us cannot maintain the balancing act of preventing insolvency forever.

It is through this long and dangerous series of events – an evolution to Bankism – that the Fed progressively lost its control of the economy and is no longer able to steer the business cycle as in yesteryear when monetary channels and fiscal incentives still functioned effectively. The economy is now incredibly dependent upon rising debt to keep it afloat, but that debt is having less and less of a stimulating effect and the debt dependency makes raising interest rates dangerous. Even with the huge new amount of debt entering the economy, the spending ability of U.S. citizens has been lagging behind so its stimulus effect from yesteryear is nowhere in sight. Adding fire to the brew, the government QE and low interest rate policies have also totally decimated the savings of average Americans, leaving millions in even more precarious and financially vulnerable positions than before while facing the threat of impeding job losses due to a weakening economy. It has also killed capital.

The problems and risks facing the American economy are now centered on the accumulated debt overhang from all the past episodes of stimulus. Debt issuance no longer stimulates very well so countries around the world are trying to stimulate their economies through currency devaluation to sell more exports and keep their economies humming. There is an ongoing currency war for trade so that countries can sell more of their goods and services via lower prices.

The U.S. is limited in what it can do to alter its currency in this regard. With the debt overhang now threatening, there is not as much maneuvering room to play games as in the past. America needs foreign nations to continue buying its U.S. bonds so that it can keep its domestic game afoot, thus financing itself with foreign funds, but those foreign nations are decreasing their demand. Will they increase or decrease their purchases if the United States depreciates its currency?

History suggests that the U.S. might one day be unable to pay all its swelling debts, which is another reason foreign nations wish to eschew American Treasury bonds.

Even though some argue that this is a remote possibility many rightfully fear that someday all this excessive U.S. money printing and debt issuance will surely end badly. In effect we have a bankrupt nation insisting that its bankruptcy remain hidden as well as the foundation of world economic policy. Do you see the risks?

To not just retire toxic debt but pump up the demand for U.S. bonds, which supports the value of the dollar, we have had the QE program of debt monetization operating at full throttle and progressing through various versions. Unknown to most, the primary purchaser of U.S. debt is probably the ESF and financial derivative machinery to hold interest rates low and glue the entire system together, which produces artificial fake demand for U.S. Treasury bonds and bills. This precarious situation cannot last long.

The U.S. financial problems are so severe that all of this truth is never spoken. Consider just some of the risks. Trust in the debt-laden dollar is waning because the Petrodollar status is at risk, there are assaults by China and Russia trying to dump its usage in trade, alternative payment mechanisms are being created that bypass the dollar, faith is declining in the ability for the U.S. to pay for all its growing debt, and the dollar's global reserve status is at risk. Nothing lasts forever in the world. The dominance of the dollar – the King Dollar era – is actually ending. This is what the interest in gold and all the cryptocurrencies is about. They are a vote of non-confidence in the dollar - an anti-dollar investment.

In the future it is certain that the majority of global trade payments will not rest singly in US dollars. Furthermore, U.S. Treasury bonds will not be the major form of banking reserves held by foreign nations either. As a result, *the United States has to start planning for a new future NOW* instead of continually relying on military interventions to thwart than inevitable outcome while blindly hoping for the best. There is a good reason that CENTCOM – The United States Central Command – has headquarters in the Mideast. It's all about maintaining the Petrodollar, which is maintained through military threats. Nevertheless, the Petrodollar is dying. If the Petrodollar goes bust then the purpose of our military presence across the world goes with it.

When OPEC nations stop accepting only US dollars for their oil because governments start paying for oil in renminbi, Euro and other currencies, this will be the final nail in the Petrodollar coffin. China is actively working to move away from the fifty-year old Petrodollar, and one day oil nations may well say "we'd rather get Euros because they are less dangerous than the dollar" or "we'd rather get renminbi because it's more stable since the U.S. is printing money to monetize its debt like Africa does."

A dying Petrodollar will remove U.S. Treasury bond buyers from the marketplace (as will lower oil prices because of a global depression), in which case the United States will have to look for alternative means of funding its expenses. It will no longer be able to use its credit card to finance its plans and programs. It will also have to start selling more real things to the outside world once again, but what would it produce to keep its trade balance in check? Would natural gas sales be enough? Of course not, so crisis looms ahead.

American consumerism, wherein Americans use borrowed cash to buy domestic and foreign goods, has served for decades as the engine of world commerce, but this will also change if there is a collapse in the value of the dollar. A time of great adjustment is at hand, an adjustment that will be fierce and painful, but a new equilibrium will eventually be found in time without dollar dominance. In that new future the dollar will no longer be supreme. The solution might even be a return to the gold standard.

5
DOMESTIC BANKING SOLUTIONS

The focus on financialization, financial engineering and the delusionary emphasis on a services-based economy rather than manufacturing has led to Bankism, which is when government authorities promote the welfare of the nation's banks over the welfare of its citizens.

In Bankism it doesn't matter what happens to the ordinary citizen as long as the health and profits of banks are kept safe at his expense.

Under Bankism it doesn't matter what happens to the greater economy as long as banks become economically immune from the consequence of bad decisions, such as bloated toxic debt loads accumulated by their own mistakes.

Under Bankism the government focuses on keeping the big banks out of insolvency and lets them become ever larger while letting others fail.

Under Bankism, every piece of banking legislation works towards making banks ever larger, more profitable and more powerful while increasing the risks to the health of the economy of real producers.

The Fed through its emphasis on Bankism has now become a rogue element within the economy. It is actually an element now undermining the economy. Over the past decade the Federal Reserve and other central banks worldwide have had to cut interest rates to historically low levels while expanding their balance sheets with bad debts to keep banks alive and avoid a depressionary collapse. Rather than reform the banks they have desperately been trying to maintain the status quo.

The financial interventions of the central banks have created all sorts of unsolvable economic pathologies and imbalances. Debt levels and money printing have soared tremendously beyond any historical bounds. In fact, the Federal Reserve has so mismanaged monetary policy that interest rate normalization is now virtually impossible despite assurances to the contrary.

With low interest rates pension funds and insurance companies cannot fund their liabilities to stay solvent so they are being forced into buying junk bond investments. Central banks are thus being pressured to raise interest rates back to normal but are worried about economies collapsing if they do, and also if they don't. Raising rates might blow up the world financial system because debt has soared everywhere and higher rates might plunge us into a depression. Savers are therefore receiving no interest on their bank deposits and are finding it difficult to live. Retirees, who are set to increase in number, will find it extra difficult to live without higher interest rates too.

Interest rates nevertheless must stay low. At the same time, the U.S. economy has itself reached a point of multiple stage economic breakdown due to many forms of internal weakening especially due to the lessening importance of the Petrodollar. A broad-scale economic breakdown will soon be the reality for the nation.

We cannot get out of this predicament. For instance, we cannot grow our way out of all the debt we are in so the Federal Reserve only has two choices: to let the debt default or inflate away all the debt by even more money printing. In this predicament, historically governments have always chosen monetary inflation. Inflation reduces a government's future obligations by enabling it to repay its debts with depreciating currency. Unfortunately this type of disguised insolvency often turns into hyperinflation.

The amount of leverage in the world right now is so astronomically high that central banks, including the Federal Reserve, cannot maintain the current trajectory of government borrowing much longer. It has to stop, but if central bankers get off the debt treadmill then many world economies will collapse. The U.S. is particularly afflicted by this debt dilemma. Furthermore, because global government debt is losing its stimulus impact central bankers will be completely out of ammo during the next recession. At that time, if not sooner, there will certainly be a massive blowup in the markets, and wise investors cognizant of the risks are already looking to precious metals investments or cryptocurrencies as insurance. The current system is unsustainable but central bankers don't want to admit it.

No one knows what will fix the global financial and monetary mess we are now in. The central banks have used up all their bullets. Government deficits are exploding, low interest rates are destroying economies, technology is disrupting jobs, currencies are tumbling, and debt-based stimulus no longer works as it once did. Governments have turned to boom and bust cycles for stimulus, mistaking unsustainable short-term gains for real economic growth. The booms and busts will get progressively bigger and bigger but one day a bust will be so big that the system will essentially fail from all of the accumulated problems.

What can we do to try and rectify the financial system to prevent this? There are several cures to the banking ills we should consider.

REINSTATE THE GLASS-STEAGALL ACT

Glass-Steagall was one of our previous protections that needs to be reinstituted. It is a regulatory safeguard that for six decades reduced the risks in the banking system by separating commercial banking (which takes deposits and makes loans) from investment banking (which underwrites and makes markets for securities). The separation of depository banking from investment banking produced a long period of prosperous stability in the financial sector that prevented harmful excesses.

This important firewall started weakening in the 1980s and then was completely dismantled in 1999 with the Gramm-Leach-Billey Act. Just eight years after Glass-Steagall was repealed the banking system blew up, threatening the world economy. As a result, U.S. taxpayers were forced to come up with $750 billion dollars, which is larger than the Pentagon's budget, in order to bail out the banking problems. This large sum was still insufficient so the Federal Reserve had to step in and expand its balance sheet by an additional $4 trillion in order to protect the solvency of banks declared "too big to fail."

Just what had Glass-Steagall previously done to prevent this? It had separated the public's money from the bankers' own speculative transactions. It had ensured that banks kept their basic lending functions separate from risky trading activities that used your money. When the disciplinary rule of Glass-Steagall was removed, it resulted in bankruptcies that caused the 99% to bailout the rich 1% of financial lords and banking elites who had made bad bets. In consequence, the mega-rich have become even richer and there has been an unprecedented explosion in American income and wealth inequality. The polarization of rich and poor has introduced political and economic instability into the nation.

Together with the loss of American manufacturing, the

repeal of Glass-Steagall, the explosion of financial debt and the excessive financialization in its wake, the balance of wealth and income in American society was basically destroyed. It turned the United States, a somewhat egalitarian democracy with a large middle class, into a nation with large income inequality. The bailouts have ended up pitting the 1% financial elite against the common man as well as destroyed the American monetary system and the image of the U.S. as an open prosperous society.

The taxpayer insured deposits of commercial banking should never serve as backing for risky bank trading activities or the creation of risky financial instruments such as financial derivatives. The U.S. government understood this in earlier times, but no longer did when Glass-Steagall was repealed. This deterioration in government competence has cost America dearly. The crash of 2008 certainly had its roots in the deregulation of the early 1980s and the congressional repeal of Glass-Steagall, both of which have loaded the economy with asset bubbles unrelated to the real on-the-ground economy of trading or making things.

By merging commercial banking with investment banking, the repeal of Glass-Steagall greatly increased the capability of the banking system to cause its own demise. It let the banking system seek profits by creating risky financial instruments that have already led to the ordinary 99% bailing out the elite 1%. Today the situation is even worse because the previous problems have not been corrected. The banks are still leveraged to the hilt, have not yet returned to their previous practices of prudent lending, have been freed from the discipline of mark-to-market valuation of their balance sheet collateral, have lost the guiding discipline of open market interest rates (due to excessive Fed intervention with ZIRP), and "too big to fail" has freed them from the fear of losses.

The best summary? Banking is a risky business whose systemic impact permeates the entire economy. It makes sense to separate commercial banking from investment banking because of those risks. We need to once again promote the long-term stability of the banking system by restoring Glass-Steagall. If, or shall we say "when" the banking, financial, monetary or economic system collapses authorities will have to do this anyway, so it is best to take all prudent steps to prevent it from happening by doing this now.

Even industry veterans, including former Citigroup CEO John Reed, believe the Glass-Steagall separation is wise. In a 2009 letter to the New York Times, Reed wrote: "Some kind of separation between institutions that deal primarily in the capital markets and those involved in more traditional deposit-taking and working-capital finance makes sense."

Glass-Steagall was originally meant to restrict banks from making certain types of speculative investments that don't benefit their customers. If reinstated it will force them to become banks once again and make their profits through lending, which is good for the economy. In short, we should forbid banks from engaging in speculative activities for profits. Banks must be encouraged to return to their original function that aids industrial and commercial development thus producing jobs for the economy.

After the Great Depression of the 1930s we restored integrity to the financial system by reforming banking regulations through measures such as Glass-Steagall. This time around we have still not restored stability to the financial system primarily because the proper financial reform efforts of many dedicated legislators and regulators have been diluted and delayed by the powerful banks, which have become too big in their influence. This needs to change.

BREAKUP LARGE BANKS INTO SMALL BANKS

In this era of Bankism, the large banks have grown too large, becoming so big that they have undue powers. Their size threatens the economy if they become insolvent, and therefore they must be reduced in size. They have become so large that the government now considers them "too big to fail," which is a contradiction of the laws of competition that keep the system of capitalism honest and of benefit to everyone.

"Too big to fail" goes hand in hand with "too risky to exist" within the broader economy, "too dangerous for the public welfare," "too big to manage," and "too big to regulate." If banks get that large then your policy has truly failed. Too big to fail banks should never have been allowed to get that large and entail systemic risks so great and deadly that they must be broken up so that they are "too small to save."

Under capitalism, the normal procedure is that businesses which make mistakes and lose money fail in bankruptcy. They go out of business and then their misused resources are released to others who can use them more profitably. Society does not need to bail businesses out because they are supposed to fail after acting unwisely, and their resources will then be redeployed elsewhere more effectively.

Consider that the giant banks and financial conglomerates would not even exist without the generous dispensations of the government and the tireless activities of many well-compensated lobbyists. They have become bigger than what is natural because they rely on the safety net of a federal bailout system. Legislative lobbying has also made them far larger, risker and more dangerous to society than could ever happen on their own. They are unnaturally large because they depend on Big Brother, the federal government, mitigating any of the risks they take on to earn profits. Should not their size then be subject to safety restrictions?

Breaking up the banks will go a long way to improving

their governance. If you break Citibank or Bank of America into many smaller banks then having smaller banks will simplify economic risk management. Internally they probably will be better managed since too big to fail also means too big to manage.

When a bank is too big to fail this means that its own failure, via interlinkages with other banks, can cause a cascading effect of subsequent banking failures that will imperil a national economy, perhaps even with international ramifications. Such a systemic risk is so large that it can only be stopped with a government bailout, meaning at public expense. Former U.S. Attorney General Eric Holder even admitted that the U.S. Justice Department was hesitant to bring criminal charges against the big banks because through their interconnectedness this could endanger the national economy. However, this explanation for refusing to pursue charges when banks do criminal wrong was, is and always will be a bunch of horse manure.

Since the big banks are all interconnected and their positions intertwined their fates are tied together like a common millstone around their necks. When one finally goes down many western financial firms will collapse with it in the contagion. The government wants to prevent this, but hasn't done anything to make the system less risky in this regard. Reducing the size of the big banks, however, does so.

Breaking up the large banks will certainly reduce the potential for them to damage the broader economy when they make mistakes. On the other hand, banks that are always backed by the government (being too big to fail) will have the perennial incentive to take on unwise risky bets because they know they will be bailed out if a problem arises, and any losses will be born by the public without any bankers privately getting into trouble. They will always engage in reckless practices for profits that ultimately threaten their solvency and then the greater economy.

There is another benefit to breaking up the larger banks too. The advantage is that it will reduce their power over politics by contracting their asset bases, and thus lessen their influence over the regulatory process they are gaming to make profits as assured as taxes.

The two big objectives we should legislatively pursue to protect the country are to once again separate commercial banking (deposit taking) from investment banking (securities operations) and place a cap on bank size. Commercial banks should not be conducting investment banking and investment banks should not be conducting commercial banking. As to bank size, it would be capped according to some such rule like "no bank will be permitted to have assets or liabilities in excess of the smallest or average gross domestic product of the fifty states." Such rules are easy to derive.

OTHER REFORMS

Reinstating Glass-Steagall to separate commercial banking (deposit taking) and investment banking (securities operations) and breaking up the large banks to end "too big to fail" (replacing it with "too small to save") are two major cornerstones to reforming the banking system.

Pursuing criminal charges against erring executives is another little spoken but "must do" reform necessary as well. Ensuring that bank assets are marked-to-market at the close of each business day, and that banks do not hold "off balance sheet" assets are other disciplinary measures that will force banks to manage solvency issues rather closely.

The repetitive cycle of bankers ignoring the principles of prudence and then once again recklessly endangering the economy through their actions shows that banks should not be allowed to engage in proprietary trading as well as basic lending. A short list of some reforms that can further reduce such recklessness to help prevent future financial catastrophes due to the banking system includes the following:

1. Ban the securitization of loans since this is what caused the monetary meltdown that bled across the world putting the whole financial system at risk back in 2008-2009. Banks should be regulated by law to keep all loans (or a majority) they make on their own books, which will then insure that banks care about the creditworthiness of the loans. This will reduce the systemic risk that previously devastated the financial system in the 2008 meltdown. If institutional investors object that they want to invest in a portfolio of long-term bank loans then they should simply buy a particular bank's CDs.

Banks should only be allowed to lend directly to borrowers, and then service and keep those loans on their own books. There are substantial real costs to the government regarding the regulation and supervision of banks selling their loans to third parties. Furthermore, there are severe consequences for the failure to adequately regulate and supervise those secondary market activities too. In other words, allowing banks to create and then sell their loans creates geometrically growing regulatory burdens as well as severe social costs whenever there are regulatory and supervisory lapses. Where is the public benefit in all this just so that banks can make more profits?

For this reason banks should be prohibited from engaging in any (or most types of) secondary market activity for their loans. The argument that these areas might be profitable for the banks is no reason to allow them to do it, nor is it a reason to extend government sponsored guarantees into those areas.

2. Convert bank capital requirements into a cash escrow requirement. Instead of a reserve composed of deposits, a bank should maintain a cash escrow reserve that should

come out of the bank's own equity and should be senior to all of the banks obligations other than insured deposits.

The problem with "bank capital" is that it is an accounting construct that can always be gamed and *it is* usually gamed by the banks and other financial institutions who are required to have one. Instituting a cash escrow can remove any gaming since cash is real and verifiable. This type of requirement will therefore make the banking system far safer. As to the proper amount, the cash escrow can easily be set as a percentage of insured deposits loans.

In addition to this, the Financial Stability Oversight Council should assess the large, risky banks with an additional capital surcharge above what regulators currently assess in order to again make failure less likely or more manageable. Being too big or too interconnected to fail in government eyes gives banks an advantage that their failures will be subsidized and they won't have to pay for any of the costs that they might pose to the economy. A surcharge would help correct for the market distortions that otherwise would favor such banks. In other words, a surcharge would force banks to internalize the true cost of their risks and thereby improve economic efficiency, while somewhat insulating taxpayers from the costs of failed institutions. The surcharge requirements should be graduated according to institution size or risk rather than set to a specific level.

In addition to converting bank capital requirements into cash requirements, the latest laws authorize the FDIC to confiscate customers' deposits to recapitalize failed banks. By new laws, a bank now owns your money and not you. Even though you deposit funds into a bank, you are now an unsecured creditor to the bank. Your money in your bank account in your name is not your money!

This law must also be changed. Because of legal cases involving MF Global and the Chicago futures brokerage Sentinel Management, we have now got court cases basically saying that private accounts in brokerage firms, even if they are segregated, can be taken over by those financial entities. This also has to change.

3. We must explore banking alternatives to diversify the banking system such as the establishment of publicly owned state banks and federal postal banks. Because of systemic riskiness, we need to experiment with non-standard banking alternatives such as community banks to complement our current system.

Postal banks, which are popular in many other nations, can solve some of our problems by serving the 38% of the American population which lacks access to mainstream banks. They can service the 30 million Americans who are either unbanked or underbanked offering services to the poor. Almost every other developed country in the world employed this solution with their post offices. Public state banks have been a cornerstone of prosperity in many countries as well and will help reduce public debt, so they should also be set up in all states besides North Dakota.

4. The fact that American consumers have reached "peak debt" and are suffering under unpayable debt loads means that Congress should amend the current Bankruptcy Code so that the public does not become a nation of debt slaves. We must allow bankruptcy to wipe out student loan debts as well as enable homeowners to restructure their underwater mortgages through the bankruptcy courts.

5. We should impose a financial transactions tax to stem the volatility of the financial markets caused by financial firms leveraging their free money to trade those markets. Such a tax will help to turn short-term trading tendencies into longer-term market outlooks better suited for supporting national prosperity trends.

A financial transactions tax would not just discourage the disruptive behavior of high frequency trading activities that are distorting the markets and true price discovery (such as by artificially lifting asset prices into new bubbles), but also the participation of banks in these efforts. Several countries already have a financial transactions tax, which may be one of the very best means for increasing long-term risk-taking in the economy and reducing its dependence on the financial sector.

There is another strategic importance to this task as well, which is that it would lessen the attractiveness of careers in finance whose compensation levels are too high. The U.S., as an economic concern, actually needs more of its best minds to go into manufacturing and innovation to help rejuvenate the nation. Reducing the importance of the financial industry through a transactions tax that also lengthens its longer term outlook would help to make this happen. Changing executive stock options to force managers to focus on longer-term prospects would also do the same thing. Dropping quarterly reports by Wall Street and replacing them with semi-annual reports would also help accomplish the same mission.

There are many other domestic reforms necessary to help fix the U.S. banking system so as to make it safe again. Since the 2008 banking meltdown we haven't made a single *real* constructive move towards remedying the banking system of its abuses. Therefore this short list should be considered just an initial elaboration upon the idea of separating depository banking from investment banking and ending "too big to fail" and "too big to jail." In short, we must:

- Separate commercial banking from investment banking
- Break up the large banks into banks "too small to save" so that they cannot blackmail the nation; the mega-banks have to be broken up into smaller banks
- Liquidate the big, broken insolvent banks

- Prosecute banks and bankers for crimes (have the prosecutors answer to the state rather than federal government in cases) and end the ability to deduct legal settlements and fees as a cost of business
- Prevent former Wall Street bakers from participating in federal or state financial regulatory bodies to prevent lobbying, favors and conflicts of interest
- Require all banking assets to be marked-to-market every day
- Reform the bankruptcy laws so that individuals can escape the fate of becoming debt slaves to the banking system forever
- Encourage alternatives to the current banking system to arise such as postal banks and public banks

The last remedy is the most important, yet perhaps the most impossible. Banks have such power, and will continue to have such power, because they donate tremendous sums of money to politicians for their political campaigns. This is all due to a Supreme Court decision – *Citizens United v. Federal Election Commission* 558 U.S. 310 (2010) – which determined that corporations had the right to give as much money as they liked to political candidates.

This in turn has led to unlimited election contributions by corporations, who now control the election process rather than the nation's citizenry. This is not what America's founder intended. With their new political power, corporations ask for more tax cuts, more deregulation and more exemption from prosecution. Only if this ruling is changed through new legislation can we ever hope to see an end to the abuses that Bankism has produced and will continue producing into the future.

6
INITIATING NEW PROSPERITY

The precarious situation we have fallen into due to monetary mismanagement necessitates that the global economic system must be revamped. Debt loads have to be cleared away and the financial system needs to be rebooted. Economies must be given clear paths to prosperity that no longer depend on financialization but on production. The Keynesian idea that the debt load doesn't matter has been revealed for the nonsense it is, and must now be abandoned for more rational thinking that might put us on a new path to prosperity. The US dollar empire is fading into the twilight, and a new system is trying to take its place to protect all parties interested in a better system of international trade.

China is clearly a superpower with a strong manufacturing base, whether it wants that distinction or not. It has determined that to protect and power its future economy it must stop depending on its previous manufacturing-supplier relationship with Europe and the Americas. It has decided to undertake the One Belt, One Road development effort that will tap into and even create an entirely new region of consumers for its goods in Eurasia.

This New Silk Road, which will create a permanent trade route connecting China, Africa and Europe, will require a tremendous amount of construction projects in infrastructure as well as countless business investments. Railways, bridges, roads, ports, mines and factories will all have to be constructed along the proposed pathway, thus opening up impoverished regions to the world economy. Incomes in these regions will soar, and the people will then turn to buying Chinese goods. Factories in these regions will also be owned by the Chinese.

The development effort of the New Silk Road will require hundreds of billions if not multi-trillions in investments. China means to grab a large share of the eventual contracts so as to power its economy for the coming decades. Against U.S. wishes, many other nations have climbed aboard the project knowing of its economic potential to enrich their own economies through lucrative contracts and new trade possibilities. Only the U.S., seeing its position of hegemon weaken, is stupid enough to refuse participation and stand aside.

In developing countries (underdeveloped nations) it is typical for infrastructure development to precede economic development; new highways, railways, bridges, airports, power lines, telecommunications and the internet make transportation and communication routes possible that blossom an underdeveloped economy. As you put them in place, along comes more of the enormous investment for actual brick and mortar businesses to supply burgeoning demand such as factories, manufacturing facilities and large fabrication plants.

China has rightly deduced that local consumer spending along the One Belt, One Road pathway, which will surely involve billions in China-supplied products, will boom. The multi-decade effort will put countless Chinese people to work, which helps to solve the employment problem for China's growing population. It is too bad that the U.S. is not so far-sighted. More importantly, Chinese citizens will be put to work in a constructive manner-that will help both the local economies they touch *and* China, thus winning goodwill.

Through this project China will create countless future buyers for its products and keep its small factories and larger manufacturing facilities operational. By developing others China is ensuring its own prosperity through solid economic development. It will do things in such a way as to win friends in foreign countries whereas the U.S. usually just threatens foreign nations. As opposed to the U.S. and much of the West it has chosen the path of manufacturing and production for prosperity rather than the paper path of financialization. Furthermore China is making moves to eliminate the US dollar in all its undertakings to avoid any possible default of toxic U.S. debt that would then destroy China's own balance sheet and economy. As part of those preparations, China is buying thousands of tons of gold.

TRUMP'S INFRASTRUCTURE STIMULUS PLAN

Now let us turn to the United States' plan for its future economic development and compare. Taking its pulse, the U.S. is in the following situation. The fact that domestic industry has left American shores is reminiscent of Third World conditions. Its banking integrity is now reminiscent of the Third World too. It has also spent trillions on warfare that has produced nothing but burgeoning expenses and an ever increasing debt load. Because it faces no serious enemies, its bloated military budget creates jobs but contributes nothing to either security or prosperity.

Over the past few decades, the typical U.S. cure for economic stimulus has turned away from manufacturing towards a combination of asset bubble inflation and putting cash in consumers' pockets through loans with the hope that the economy will respond.

With consumers out of work (or just fearful of losing their jobs) and already laden with the maximum debt possible, this remedy no longer works. Logic dictates that it will also continue to fail into the future. Putting money in people's pockets for consumption doesn't do anything as far as building the economy anymore since most products are now made overseas. Something new must be tried.

President Trump has therefore proposed (1) to imitate the Chinese New Silk Road by undertaking a massive domestic infrastructure spending plan, and (2) bring jobs back home while creating new ones through tariffs, tax incentives and deregulation. Both of these stimulus ideas are confronted with problems. Let us take a look at the infrastructure proposal first.

When we talk about the state of U.S. infrastructure, the first common fallacy is that U.S. *federal* infrastructure is dilapidated, collapsing or crumbling. Washington's primary infrastructure responsibility is maintaining the Interstate Highway System, and it is actually in pretty good shape (including its heavily trafficked bridges). The national infrastructure system is fine.

When we go to the states, however, we find a different story. For instance, of the one-hundred most heavily trafficked U.S. bridges in need of serious repair, 80% are located in California. This is then a state matter; the problem belongs to California and not the federal government. There is no reason why the taxpayers of other states should be paying for the upkeep of California's bridges, roads and highways or even sewers. Dwight D. Eisenhower, in setting up the Interstate Highway System, pointed out that 99% of road surfaces should be a nonfederal responsibility, and most infrastructure needs are truly local in nature. The problem of failing infrastructure therefore falls largely on the doorstep of local and state governments rather than Washington.

Intrastate infrastructure spending is more properly managed and paid for by state and local governments anyway, being funded by local users and taxpayers. Since about 95% of infrastructure investment – roads, streets, bridges, airports, ports, mass transit, sewers, etc. – is overwhelmingly local in nature it should be paid for by local taxes and user fees. To avoid saddling the public with productivity-draining costs for decades you must do this cheaply and wisely. The best financing to repair the nation's infrastructure should be arranged as a form of "self-liquidating" debt.

Now let's turn to the possible long-term fiscal stimulus effect President Trump thinks might transpire due to federal infrastructure spending, which is not the type of fiscal stimulus that America actually needs. Aside from any pros, you must recognize that this would dump even more long-term debt on Americans whose debt load is already astronomically high due to the mistakes of the Federal Reserve and banking system.

First, the cold facts are that infrastructure spending will simply not cause factories to sprout up in a nation that has outsourced its manufacturing base to lower-cost countries. There are no reasons that infrastructure spending will rebuild economic activity or competitiveness in a developed nation like the United States, so once any money is spent on infrastructure construction its stimulus effect will be gone. Infrastructure spending may be necessary to conduct repairs or create new facilities, but it doesn't really render a competitive cost advantage or boost regional productivity.

Second, the plan requires an incredible amount of low-cost financing that Trump may not be able to secure without the cooperation of Wall Street, which will seek its normal plunder and profit in various fees and interest. The danger is saddling the public with productivity-draining costs for decades for projects that do not produce any long-term economic stimulus. China's infrastructure plan actually stimulates its economy for decades due to the U.S. infrastructure plan does not!

If Trump really thought he could get long-term domestic economic stimulus from increased infrastructure spending, to prevent a multi-generational burden he needs lower-cost funding from a new type of debt and new type of bank. A new type of bank will actually cure many of the prosperity ills of America in the long-run.

History gives us a clue as to what should work. The populist President Andrew Jackson, who was at war with the nation's biggest bankers, already set the precedent. Jackson shut down the Second Bank of the United States in 1833, which was the country's national bank holding a position roughly equivalent to the Federal Reserve. The First National Bank had been created by George Washington and Alexander Hamilton in 1791 as a central depository for federal funds. In 1816 the Second Bank of the United States was thereafter run by directors with strong ties to manufacturing and industry.

President Jackson didn't like the fact that the Second Bank focused mainly on the urban and northern industrial states because he wanted it to expand into the unsettled western regions where people were moving. He wanted that particular region of the country to grow and flourish. In catering its loans to other areas, Jackson felt that the Second Bank, which was run by a privileged class of businessmen, oppressed the will of the common people.

Is this not reminiscent of the complaints heard today? Do we not often hear that the U.S. monetary authorities are catering to a privileged class of bankers and financiers (the 1% elite) who are profiting from the Fed while ignoring the citizenry? It is said that the best bank is to store the nation's wealth among the people, but the U.S. is taking the opposite approach in its plan to generate prosperity.

In 1833 the populist Jackson removed all federal funds

from the Second Bank of the United States and redistributed it to various state banks. A similar plan might be done today, thus rejuvenating the nation, if a series of public state banks were set up along the pattern of the Bank of North Dakota. As the bank's President Eric Hardmeyer explained:

Our funding model, our deposit model is really what is unique as the engine that drives that bank. And that is we are the depository for all state tax collections and fees. And so we have a captive deposit base, we pay a competitive rate to the state treasurer. And I would bet that that would be one of the most difficult things to wrestle away from the private sector—those opportunities to bid on public funds. But that's only one portion of it. We take those funds and then, really what separates us is that we plow those deposits back into the state of North Dakota in the form of loans. We invest back into the state in economic development type of activities. We grow our state through that mechanism.

In the last decade China has actually funded a portion of its 12,000 miles of high-speed rail through a similar system. About 40% of Chinese railway bonds were issued by the Ministry of Railways. Another 40-50% came from loans by federally-owned banks while 10-20% came from local governments.

The Chinese government banks, like private banks in the U.S., generated the loans by creating money (credit) on their books. The Chinese banks also return their profits to the Chinese government, thus making the loans interest-free and able to be rolled over indefinitely.

Basically, for certain infrastructure projects the Chinese government decides what it wants, its banks create the credit on the government's credit card, the construction companies, suppliers and workers are paid because of the credit, and the loans are repaid with the proceeds.

The U.S. should follow this model too because it will dramatically cut fiscal costs. Most people want to cut costs by privatizing infrastructure, but history proves that privatization will disastrously escalate costs in monopolistic situations. As soon as you sell public utilities to investors, for instance, they will rent them back to the public and squeeze out profits from higher user fees and tolls. This is almost always a bad deal for the public. It only provides long-term profit guarantees to private companies. To compound the pain, decades later people will be paying higher tolls for an asset that could have belonged to them all along, and which was sold simply to make some outsider rich at the public's expense.

The normal propaganda usually expounded is that private companies will build public infrastructure projects cheaper than the government, but the truth is that private contractors typically charge more than twice what the government would have paid federal workers for the same job.

As proposed, a perfect solution for the nation is a publicly-owned bank, one for each state, with the Bank of North Dakota (BND) being the model example. Although a public state-owned institution, the Bank of North Dakota is even more profitable than Goldman Sachs, has a better credit rating than J.P. Morgan Chase, and has seen solid profit growth for almost 15 years despite recent economic downswings. Even when North Dakota was experiencing the oil bust the bank was still profitable because of its business model.

BND does not pay bonuses, fees or commissions. It has no high paid executives. It does not have multiple branches or need to advertise. It does not speculate on derivatives. It does not have private shareholders seeking short-term profits. Any profits return to the bank, which distributes them as dividends to the state.

The BND behaves exactly like a bank, but also serves

an economic development mission for the public. *It serves the citizens as the development bank for the state.* Responding to needs across the state, it is at the forefront of every major economic initiative in North Dakota. It lets the state have some control over its economic destiny by owning its own bank. Should not every state have such a public bank?

Right now North Dakota funds infrastructure projects with 2% fixed interest rate loans up to 30-year maturities. Its loans are used to construct transportation infrastructure, sewer and water lines, and even water treatment plants. If President Trump were to spend $1 trillion in infrastructure, the interest cost would be $200 billion per annum via normal lending plans. Private equity averages returns of 11.8% annually over a 10-year basis so turning his plan into private projects would require even more substantial interest.

If you want to sponsor a national infrastructure initiative the public bank plan for infrastructure loans wins. The great thing about the plan is that BND is not lending scarce state revenues. It creates new money in the form of bank credit when making the loans. By making infrastructure loans the bank essentially creates new money for the economy, just like the Fed, but that money is interest-free to the local government.

To get much-needed money into local economies for development purposes, a government should borrow money from its own bank. After receiving interest on its loans the bank should then return it to the government. This would eliminate any reliance on expensive private capital to finance public needs, avoid strapping future generations with unsustainable debt, and allow the public to retain ownership of infrastructure while cutting its costs many-fold. Public banks are the true solution to building national economies!

Unfortunately, public banks run into problems when being founded. Since they act as type of mini-Fed they represent a threat to commercial interest-earning banks.

Therefore they are always opposed by their commercial competitors seeking to protect their profits. Competition and obstructionist efforts from the entrenched banks is usually the main obstacle to a better deal for public citizens.

If the U.S. wants to rebuild local airports, bridges, tunnels, highways and other infrastructure as a form of fiscal stimulus while avoiding the sticker shock, it should establish fifty charted state institutions to deal with infrastructure loans, lowering state costs tremendously. The Trump infrastructure spending plan, as currently proposed, relies too heavily on public-private partnerships, which will surely gouge the public for stellar returns to the private partners who will also end up owning the assets in the end.

SELF-FUNDING THROUGH MONEY CREATION

The key to state public banks is that they create money without charging themselves interest, which is unlike the Fed that charges interest to the U.S. government, later returns it, but also pays a 6% dividend to itself. Is that dividend not a 6% profit? Historical precedent involving Abraham Lincoln sheds some light on what would happen if we removed this extra cost burden from the U.S. financial system.

President Lincoln once went against the entrenched banking system with its monopolistic profits and tried to create currency free of its influence. He needed money to finance the Civil War, but the bankers wanted to charge him 24% to 36% interest. Lincoln therefore passed a law authorizing the printing of full legal tender Treasury notes to pay for the war effort. These were called "Greenbacks" because they were printed with green ink on the back. Lincoln printed $449,338,902 worth of greenbacks that were debt-free and interest-free money to finance the war.

Britain freaked out when this happened. Sensing the

jeopardy of its bankers, *The London Times* wrote about the government money printing, "If that mischievous financial policy, which had its origin in the North America Republic, should become indurated down to a fixture, then that Government will furnish its own money without cost. It will pay off debts and be without a debt. It will have all the money necessary to carry on its commerce. It will become prosperous beyond precedent in the history of the civilized governments of the world. The brains and wealth of all countries will go to North America. That government must be destroyed, or it will destroy every monarchy on the globe."

When sovereign governments print interest-free and debt-free paper money it is a tremendous threat to the power of international bankers who impose this type of tax on others. Remember that the very first thing the rebel forces did in Libya, with their outside help, was to establish a new central bank under international banking influence. That's how important the issue is if you want to control the fate of a nation. A maxim summarizing this principle, often attributed to the Mayer Amschel Rothschild runs, "Let me issue and control a nation's money and I care not who writes the laws." Our own President Garfield also once said, "Whoever controls the volume of money in any country is absolute master of all industry and commerce." Incidentally, American Presidents Garfield and McKinley, who both advocated a return to the gold-standard, were assassinated in office.

In any case, after *The London Times* piece was published the British government, which was controlled by the London and European bankers, started to support the Confederate South so as to destroy Lincoln's government. The North won the war, but Lincoln was later assassinated.

Afterwards Congress revoked the Greenback Law and enacted the National Banking Act in its place, which specified that the national bank was to be *privately owned* and its bank notes were to be interest bearing. The Greenbacks were also retired from circulation as soon as they came back to the Treasury for the payment of taxes.

Although in 1972 the Treasury Department computed that by creating his own money Abraham Lincoln's issuance of $400 million in Greenbacks had saved $4 billion in interest, few question why the Federal Reserve today prints interest bearing notes in a convoluted scheme of payback. Why not simply do things the easy way and create debt-free money directly? No one can give a reasonable answer to this question, but perhaps the 6% Federal Reserve dividend would somehow be at stake.

In 1913 the Federal Reserve Act was passed that replaced the National Banking Act that had previously replaced the Greenback Law. If the United States had continued to follow the policy of Abraham Lincoln then the bankers would be out of a guaranteed way to make money and America would be a debt-free nation. We would be issuing new currency that did not bear interest and become stronger than any other nation in the world because of that single fact. Unfortunately, the Federal Reserve Act gave up the right enshrined within the United States Constitution that the United States could create its own money. Now the United States operated under a central bank that is privately owned and issues a fixed dividend.

CENTURY BONDS

If the United States experiences any sort of monetary crisis that causes interest rates to rise, funding Trump's new infrastructure plan (or any expensive government plans) will be much more costly without public banks. Another cure is to start issuing Treasury bonds of longer duration, namely 50-year, 75-year and 100-year bonds, or specifically for that purpose. The U.S. Treasury has never sold a bond with longer than a 30-year maturity, but these ultra-long bonds would solve a multitude of problems, such as locking in low long-term interest rates for project funding.

Countries like Belgium, Ireland, Austria and Mexico have already sold bonds maturing in 50, 70 or 100 years, so by issuing such bonds the U.S. would be following a proven trend. The Treasury should take advantage of the ultra-low rates we now have and issue the long-term bonds in order to benefit from the low interest costs. This type of very long-term debt issuance can fund Trump's fiscal stimulus plans nicely.

THE NEW MANUFACTURING EMPHASIS

One of the correct ideas that President Trump touted in his election campaign was that the U.S. needs to stop emphasizing Bankism and financialization as the road to economic stimulus. Instead, the U.S. needs to make a dramatic change in the country's course by bringing manufacturing back home, and with that return the good paying jobs will come back. Even though the human element of assembly is no longer as crucial as it once was, we still need things to be manufactured in the U.S. in order to create exports (foreign income), the demand for dollars, and bring down the trade deficit, all of which lower inflation. There is an urgent need to reindustrialize America by bringing back its manufacturing base.

This is one of the ideas inherent in "Make America Great Again." Manufacturing is the most important economic engine for the USA, not Bankism. Only by reviving the American manufacturing base will the necessary jobs for working middle class America return whose labor costs are already too high by international standards.

We are presently a consumer economy where 70% of our GDP is consumption-based (over two-thirds of all jobs are directly or indirectly dependent upon consumer expenditures) but the consumer no longer makes enough money to participate in that economy. Household disposable income just isn't enough anymore. Nearly 80% of Americans can no longer raise their spending levels and are maxed out with peak things at peak debt, so where will rising wages come from when nobody has any money to spend?

No economy can function if its people don't have enough money to spend. In addition, savings accounts and even pension returns have declined and without that money people cannot buy wanted widgets either. Overall, the employment among 25-54 year-olds ceased growing back in 2000 and once it stopped the U.S. had to substitute accelerating debt stimulus to maintain growth along with lowered interest rates. This no longer works.

There is only so far you can move the economy through declining interest rates and rising debt. There is only so far you can stimulate it in a healthy manner with consumer purchases. The consumer market not only lacks incomes but is already saturated – at peak stuff – in most of the developed world so the demand isn't there any more after stimulus. The loss of good jobs has even made it difficult for people to get married and form households, all of which normally produces extra consumption. Basically our monetary and fiscal foibles have gutted and destroyed countless families and communities.

As a nation we are no longer organized around making widgets but around the buying and selling of debt. We are too focused on the commodification of liabilities. When financialization took off the actual manufacturing of products fell second to the buying and selling of debt and other financial instruments. The making of products came to an end because the government chose not to protect it even though manufacturing has a multiplier effect just like banking. For every factory built, countless other jobs are multiplicatively created in the economy involving photocopiers, fax machines, fork lift trucks and so on.

Because of massive financial mismanagement by authorities, we have transitioned from a good wage economy for skilled workers who could formerly consume to a lower wage service economy, and with better jobs now gone from the general economy you cannot make up the difference except with massive amounts of debt stimulus. We made the problem even worse by systematically shifting factories, jobs, innovation and technology eastwards, thus redistributing economic power by diluting our own. The wholesome transformation of the economy has been a catastrophe.

Growth is not to be expected from a hollowed-out economy. While the banks have become more resilient as a result of government interventions to save them this has come at the cost of the larger economy, which is Bankism at its core. Though done in response to the threat of a depression, QE has even made the economy much more susceptible to the next economic downturn.

Going forward, if we now replace the workers we still have left with robots and automation, those robots will not need to buy consumer goods either. Robots don't buy houses, furniture, cars, clothing, entertainment, health services and so on. With automation looming closer at the doorstep even more low-skilled, low-paying jobs will disappear from the consumer economy, not to mention the fact that financing for Social Security and Medicare will then collapse too. Automation might force people out of certain job markets forever. The only thing that has prevented total economic collapse so far has been government intervention, but the liquidity the Fed created has been going primarily into pumping up financial assets rather than job creation, inflating the prices of assets disproportionately held by the rich. Nevertheless the economy would be stagnant without the Fed's intervention to increase consumer credit.

In short, the United States has to reverse the offshoring of American jobs. We have set up tax incentives for corporations to manufacture abroad, and they need to be eliminated to bring manufacturing back home. We cannot stimulate our way out of job losses. We require not one big major way but hundreds of little ways to increase the number of domestic manufacturers and bring jobs home again. This should be our national emergency priority program for many years running! We need a priority on domestic economic development rather than raising the Pentagon's budget. This might include a barrage of efforts such as tax credits, tariffs, regulatory waivers, industrial parks, R&D deductions, etcetera. The economy has to start making and exporting things again rather than stimulating itself through fiat paper games. Bankism has to take a back seat to the priority of making and selling things once again, especially exports. However, since both wages and taxes are lower offshore it will be nearly impossible to create competitive domestic manufacturing unless tariffs and tax code changes are instituted. These changes will have to be made carefully in consideration of the need for global competitiveness. As just one example, the payroll tax, which makes our labor uncompetitive, might be eliminated entirely and replaced with an imports and consumption tax instead. Many such alternatives must be explored.

To help make U.S. workers less expensive Trump hopes to repeal or reform the costly and unworkable Obamacare program, which has turned many full-time employees into part-time workers. Repeal would only return us to the bad old days of 2013 when the healthcare industry already sucked. To truly help people it must undo decades of government interference in health care, but at lower cost than the margins baked in for insurance companies. The single payer system might be the only solution with the cost then born by the entire nation, but can the country really afford it?

THE NEW COLLEGE EMPHASIS

The loss of industry unwilling to return home, unless legislation makes this more attractive, will require new types of industry to be built inside the United States (since more of the old would also leave again). This is unlikely to occur unless a new Kondratieff wave of innovation sprouts up that favors domestic production because of lower shipping costs or because it requires fewer people per facility. Can 3D printing be one of the solutions to the domestic manufacturing renaissance we require? No one knows.

To support the innovation that drives manufacturing and will save the nation, colleges and universities should start to switch their emphasis from business to engineering and invention such as by offering practical courses on TRIZ, a method of inventing that can be taught. The national education system should place a stronger emphasis on technical subjects that would in such a way attract the best brains into innovation and engineering. Tougher math and science requirements need to be instituted for graduation from U.S. high schools.

Laws encouraging small business entrepreneurs also need to be passed. Since small firms create most of the jobs in an economy, the emphasis in politics has to switch from the large to the small while clearing away the regulatory obstacles that hamper small biz. New technologies must also be developed that offer manufacturing opportunities. Our problem is that foreign nations now match us with their domestic educational skills as well as access to capital and technology. We have to jump ahead to create a higher level of competitive advantage that concentrates on higher value-added output. Erik Reinert's *How Rich Countries Got Rich and Why Poor Countries Stay Poor* is a good guide with lessons to that way forward.

As John Williams of ShadowStats.com points out, the real unemployment rate in the U.S. economy is closer to

23% rather than 6%. For instance, the labor force participation rate (the share of Americans actively employed or looking for work) is only around 63% and dropping, lending credence to the claim that the unemployment rate is not even at sub-10% levels. We need people back at work again at higher paying jobs, but all jobs will matter in the future.

What will be the economic wave that powers the economy going forward? Whatever it is we must return to domestically manufacturing things the world wants and become an exporter again with factories *onshore*. This is the only thing that will provide high paying domestic jobs and solid prosperity. The servicing of the fiat paper industry, with its commodification of loans and concentration on the finance sector, is not the future path of success for America. It is a pathway to Third World conditions.

Without employment there will be no consumers to power the economy or salaries to produce the tax base. Municipal and state governments, deprived of taxes, cannot make pension payments or pay for current services. If not buying U.S. exports (or if a nation can print up their own currency to buy critical commodities) there is no need for a foreign country to hold dollars in their banking system, so the dollar will decline in value and imports will rise in price unless we find a non-Bankism solution to the loss of domestic manufacturing. To avoid the fate of being a Third World country we must bring manufacturing back into our borders once again.

RECAPITALIZE WORLD FINANCIAL SYSTEM

At the same time as we attempt to reindustrialize the U.S., both the United States and the global financial system must be recapitalized and shorn of all the toxic debt that has built up that threatens it like a Sword of Damocles over our heads. Although the U.S. will not like hearing it, its debt problems are now so severe that other nations will certainly endeavor to reduce their dependence on the toxic dollar just from this single aspect alone. This is another reason that faith in the dollar is declining.

What can we do to build manufacturing up again? In the search for growth we will probably have to turn to micro-factories that are close to their markets and do not demand much labor. We will need a way to compete against lower-cost foreign labor, lower overseas tax rates and overheads, and overseas transportation costs.

The New Silk Road initiative shows one path of development, but the U.S. will probably not be able to emulate this massive effort, even with Trump's infrastructure plan. Furthermore, Trump's plan will not produce long-term jobs and exports, which just goes to show the competition we will be facing in kick-starting the nation into major exporter status once again. In fact, the U.S. should cease trying to thwart China and its development projects and join the bandwagon in order to secure valuable construction contracts from whatever it is doing.

The New Silk Road initiative, and the other efforts that China and Russia are working on to lessen world dependence on the US dollar, will most likely in time involve gold bullion as a primary reserve asset. This, in addition to fears about a dollar and Treasury bond collapse, are reasons why both nations are discharging their U.S. T-bonds and accumulating gold bullion. If and when the dollar starts to be replaced the event will coincide with a massive rise in gold and silver prices. The entire global system will change if it replaces the dollar with a modified gold standard. This is the next topic to consider.

7
THE GOLD TRADE STANDARD

A fading superpower incapable of paying its bills will be provocatively challenged by others. Therefore once the US dollar is no longer the undisputed king of currencies, the U.S. is sure to be challenged on multiple fronts. Right now the U.S. is being challenged economically by China since it has become the manufacturer of the world. The U.S. will also probably be challenged militarily in the Mideast, such as by Iran and Russia, if it insists on applying its usual practice of using military weapons to maintain the dying Petrodollar standard.

No country retains the global currency reserve status forever. We cannot even say that paper currencies "last long" since the track record of fiat currencies that failed is near 100%. Nearly every one goes belly up over time. One day, this too will certainly be the fate of US dollar since it hasn't been granted the boon of perpetuity either. Nothing in existence can withstand the law of impermanence, so the U.S. is in a constant battle against the fact that the world's reserve currency has, can and will change over time, especially when that country makes strategic mistakes in its financial, economic and military spheres.

This fact foretells of the inevitable doom for the dollar's status one day, but you simply don't know when it will occur. It could take years, decades or centuries but it is only a matter of time before the global reserve currency once again changes due to overwhelming circumstances. There will eventually come a day where there will be a global currency reset to replace the Petrodollar standard, thus reducing the need for US dollar usage in banking and trade. That's when the eventual replacement of the dollar as the world's reserve currency is likely to happen.

Perhaps the catalyst for the demise of the dollar standard will be the rise of cryptocurrencies which embody escape routes from the clutches of the central banking system. The cryptocurrencies have become increasingly attractive because of fears that there might be another major financial downturn/crisis, and the central banks will then restrict the movement of cash within the banking system. If governments are ever successful in banning cash (besides just restricting its movement) it will make negative interest rates easier because you won't be able to take your money out of the bank. The banks will then be able to just subtract negative interest rates out of your savings accounts. Bitcoin helps protect you against this potential outrage. Unfortunately, its weakness is a dependence upon the existence of computers, the internet and electricity.

Perhaps the catalyst for the demise of the dollar will be an eastern gas cartel that accepts non-dollar payments, such as what Russia is working on with Iran and Qatar. Perhaps it will be the fact that Venezuela now accepts renminbi for its oil and other countries will follow.

Maybe it will be an oil benchmark price controlled by China, which might replace the oil-backed dollar with a gold-backed system. Right now China, the world's top oil consumer, is preparing to launch a crude oil futures contract denominated in renminbi and convertible to gold. It will be the first Chinese commodity contract open to foreign investment funds, trading houses and oil firms. This is extraordinarily dangerous for the US dollar. A momentous event, it will break the dollar's hold on oil sales because it will allow foreign firms to trade oil in the renminbi or gold and thus bypass any US dollar sanctions. All of the BRICS nations have already endorsed China's oil-to-renminbi-to-gold plan.

Once China gets going with backing the oil trade with gold-linked renminbi (yuan) then its control over the eastern oil trade will broaden and solidify. It may even lead to Chinese control of the non-eastern oil trade over time. This is a gigantic threat to the fate of the US dollar because other trade flows may follow. If global oil trade, or a large proportion of world oil trade, turns to gold, other trade will most likely follow.

Aside from these facts that (1) fiat currencies eventually go bust and that (2) reserve currencies change over time, you must also understand that (3) every few decades *the reigning monetary system in the world also fails in some overall way* and has to be reengineered to restore confidence to the system so that it can get going again.

This is not opinion but rather just a historical fact. Monetary scholar Edwin Vieira has pointed out that every 30-40 years the reigning monetary system usually fails in some way and then has to be retooled to start again. Author Jim Rickards has identified three times within the last 100 years alone - namely in 1914, 1939, and 1971 – where the international monetary system collapsed and had to be changed. Every few decades it certainly has had to be reset.

What will the next reset look like? The Petrodollar monopoly will certainly fade away as countries start to transact oil in other currencies. Due to less need for it, the dollar will then embark on a multi-year road of decline while countries stop buying U.S. Treasury bills and bonds due to lesser usage. This reinforcing trend will cause the dollar to drop in value even further. An increasing number of nations will then turn to non-dollar trade payments, accentuating the trend in global dollar rejection. Barter may substantially increase and develop into a substantial amount of world trade. Although the dollar will decline in importance, world trade however will always need some sort of standard in-between vehicle that all trust. What will it be?

The most probable replacement candidate is the reinstallation of the gold standard for settling world trade. Another alternative is some sort of gold-backed cryptocurrency using blockchain technology, which will thus remove the need for endless shipments of precious metals across borders. This type of system would require decentralized gold hubs across the world that would serve as regional gold depositories. Perhaps regional trade unions will develop, based upon trade treaties, that will develop such institutions.

Regardless as to the form of the final system, the basic idea is that nations are turning away from using the US dollar in trade. On top of this, the U.S. might even face bond defaults sometime soon, and other nations are a bit leery of the dollar due to this possibility. A monetary default of any type involving the global reserve currency (the dollar) will be a global catastrophe *except* to those nations who have prepared by switching some of their assets to gold and silver bullion. Why the precious metals? Because they are not fiat paper instruments whose values might go to zero. Rather, they are internationally traded commodities without counterparty risk. They have historically served as the major payments vehicle for world trade and have commonly served as a store of wealth in unsafe times.

Gold and silver are actually a form of insurance against central banking foibles. If any sort of financial crisis or collapse happens that is related to central banks, people will be scrambling for assets that can hold their value. Gold and silver are two such assets. Their additional benefit is that they have historically been used as money in many instances, and can definitely be used as money again in just such situations.

There are many reasons why the world will probably turn to gold and silver, but one stands out clearest. All nations have inflated their currencies and taken on astounding debt loads they cannot repay. Every currency therefore now entails tremendous counterparty risks. Since debts that cannot be repaid won't be repaid, governments will eventually either default on their debts or try to inflate them away through currency depreciation.

Only gold and silver can maintain their value in such instances. They previously served as the global trade standard and therefore will probably do so again because their usage solves an entire host of international problems like this. The gold standard, since it is easier to administrate than a silver standard, may be in the cards.

The reasons governments don't like the gold standard, however, is because it imposes upon them financial discipline and limits their ability to wage war. From the public's perspective, however, this is exactly why it is to be preferred.

The gold standard is not about gold. It is about *backing fiat paper currency with a real commodity*. Being backed by a tangible commodity is what ultimately gives a currency value other than just the tax receipts of yet more fiat paper currency (which may in themselves turn out to be worthless). A reserve currency needs to be backed by a commodity having international value. Instead of a gold standard the US dollar is actually on a petroleum standard since it is actually backed by oil. The Petrodollar's existence has always insured that the US dollar has been backed by the commodity petroleum. Gold would just be a substitute for petroleum.

A gold standard would therefore enforce a monetary discipline on countries that they fiscally live within their means, instituting a natural discipline of austerity. U.S.

living standards would have to be downgraded and the national economy would probably deteriorate during a transition phase to a gold standard unless monetary authorities secure ample quantities of gold so as to fit into the new system. Basically the United States went off of a gold-backed currency regime of sound money onto a fiat currency system of unstable interest rates and endless money printing, and will probably have to return to gold.

The adoption of the gold standard will once again impose financial discipline on governments and limit their reckless spending. Previously under the gold standard the money printing abilities of central bankers were constrained by the discipline of gold. When money was freed of the need to be backed by gold then that's when an era of unrestrained money creation by central bankers began along with all the attendant problems. The supply of paper currency issued has not been kept limited, so it has *lost its value against gold*. Additionally, massive unrestricted government spending has over time turned the U.S. balance of payments negative, damaging the dollar and building up foreign claims against it. If we look at it from a purely accounting sense, the U.S. is now essentially broke but hiding the fact from the public.

Most every central bank is now running an expansive monetary policy that is even looser than those seen during the Great Depression, and global government debts are ever mounting worldwide as this Keynesian money printing fiasco continues unchecked. Some governments are even selling new debt in order to raise enough cash to cover their interest obligations on the old debt they previously created! When it comes to world debt, we are seeing a Ponzi scheme of enormous proportions that is ultimately destined to collapse because there is no way to pay it back or grow out of it.

The government debt levels for many nations are now so high that they can only be maintained by artificially low interest rate policies (QE quantitative easing), otherwise the nations would face systemic insolvencies since they couldn't pay higher interest on these debts. All the while, global sovereign debt levels are building ever larger due to all the excess money printing required for providing domestic liquidity and stimulus. The dam will soon break.

Let's take the case of Japan as an example. Currently the Japanese government debt levels are so large that they are mathematically impossible to be repaid. For instance, fund manager Kyle Bass has warned that Japanese debt levels are north of 20 times the government's tax revenues. The country is therefore technically insolvent. The most recent numbers show that nearly 43% of Japanese central government tax revenues are now used to pay the interest on Japan's debt. If Japan's interest rates were raised the country would certainly face insolvency. Bass flatly warns, "There's no chance at Japan repaying their debt."

Ludwig von Mises once said, "There is no means of avoiding the final collapse of a boom brought about by credit expansion (debt creation). The alternative is only whether the crisis should come sooner as the result of a voluntary abandonment of further credit expansion, or later as a final and total catastrophe of the currency system involved." This pretty much summarizes the situation that the entire world is facing because of the excesses brought on by creating so much debt. A gold standard is a remedy.

The global financial system must now be recapitalized due to all the debt that cannot be repaid and which can only be maintained so long as countries continue their ZIRP and NIRP policies. One of the new ideas is to try to remove cash from domestic banking systems so that if a collapse happens the governments can still control the populace.

Actually, there are probably many preliminary steps to a global currency reset being worked out right now by governments "just in case it happens" but those types of plans will not be laid out in full disclosure for public benefit. The final cure will most probably involve gold and silver bullion as primary reserve assets, which will coincide with a massive rise in precious metal prices.

You should know that most of the stable solutions to currency destruction that have worked in the past involved a return to asset-backed currencies, such as the gold standard, to stabilize the markets. This gives hope. When unrestricted fiat currency printing is displaced by the discipline of the precious metals once again then the entire global system will likely shed itself of toxic habits. A common objection is that there isn't enough gold to do this, but all you have to do is simply raise its price.

In 2012, billionaire Hugo Salinas or Mexico even wrote a letter to the Prime Minister of Greece, Alexis Tsipras, proposing how to solve Greek's problems by going to a silver standard. Salinas urged Tsipras to mint a new Greek silver coin, and said that this action would solve many of Greece's monetary problems. Here is what he said in his letter:

> Mr. Tsipras, the desperate situation of Greece offers you a unique opportunity to do something fundamentally great for Greece and to establish yourself as a great national leader. You are a young man and thanks to this, you have a brilliant opportunity to build a long career as a Statesman - not as a politician, but as a Statesman.
>
> In effect, the return of the Drachma would allow Greece to pull itself together once more. It would definitely not make matters worse, for the present situation is so bad that the Drachma will give Greece an immediate respite.
>
> Thus, the monetary heart of Greece would once again begin to beat and furnish the necessary liquidity to get the economy "moving" again.
>
> However, this measure will inevitably entail monetary inflation through the creation of increasing amounts of Drachma to cover the

budget deficits of the Greek government for some time, and the inflation will bring about the constant devaluation of the Drachma.

This will allow the renovation of Greek exports and a rebirth of Tourism to Greece, since Europeans will prefer to travel to Greece due to the advantages which the rate of exchange with the Drachma will offer.

However, it is clear that a permanent inflation cannot be acceptable and cannot offer political stability for Greece.

It is on this point, that I present to your government an alternative that no "accredited" economist has had the will, or the necessary understanding of human affairs to consider.

All "accredited" economists in the world will say that the Government of Greece should "eliminate the fiscal deficit" to put a stop to pernicious inflation. However, these economists are not in Government; they are not politicians or Statesmen and they ignore the huge problem of convincing a population accustomed to spending, to save money. The keynesians, who are the majority of economists today, detest the idea that the population should save; they attempt to solve all problems by increasing spending, until finally the whole economy collapses. The Greek economy has collapsed because the money to spend, which came from foreign loans in Euros, has finally dried up: there is no more money to spend.

Mr. Tsipras, the way to lead the Greek people to stability is through real money, and not through fictitious money such as the Euro, which has led to the present chaos. The present European disaster was guaranteed from the day of birth of the Euro as a fictitious - fiat - money, of a symbolic nature, and not real money.

It will be only by giving Greeks a silver coin in parallel with the Drachma, that you and your Party may gradually lead Greece to fiscal equilibrium. Your government will have to modify profoundly the mentality of the Greeks, before achieving this goal. Let us think of all the great leaders the world has seen, and we shall see that all of them governed by means of the ideas which they inspired in their nations.

With a silver coin in their power, Greeks will feel an enormous pride in Greece and there will be a renewed hope of a better future, a condition which is indispensable in order to achieve a recovery. Modern "economists" never mention "pride" and "hope" as important factors in economic matters. And, of course they are supremely important!

Thanks to a renewed pride and hope, Greeks will be better disposed to accept the measures which your government may wish to implement, and to tolerate the difficult transition to fiscal balance; a period during which your government will have to control gradually the level of expenditures and government investment, until a sustainable level is attained.

Not only this: the conservative sector of your population - for whom you will also have to govern - will watch the continual devaluation of the Drachma (necessary as a part of government planning) with disapproval, and will strive to remove you from your position, unless they see in you the Statesman that has given Greece a silver coin, which may be used by those who wish to protect their savings, and who will, in the main, be conservatives. Thus, the conservatives will want to see you remain in power, so that you may continue your policy of placing silver money in the hands of

Greeks.

The silver coin in parallel with the Drachma is the formula for national unity and reconstruction. The reconstruction of Greece will require of savings and nothing furthers saving more efficiently that silver money.

How can a silver coin be put into circulation in Greece?

I outline the basic principles:

1. The silver coin will circulate in parallel with the Drachma. The Drachma will remain the monetary unit of Greece. The silver coin will have a monetary value expressed in Drachmas. (Note as of March 17, 2015: Alternatively, the silver coin might have a monetary value expressed in terms of the Euro or of the Dollar.)

2 . Greece will coin a small silver coin, using the Greek symbols: Athene on one side, with the Owl on the other, following a tradition of thousands of years.

3. This small coin - the "Owl" - will contain 1/10 of a Troy ounce of silver, alloyed with copper to .9166 to give it hardness.

4. This coin will be assigned a monetary value by the Monetary Authority, which shall be preferably, the Greek Treasury. This coin will bear no engraved value; otherwise, the coin will go out of circulation immediately as the price of silver rises, whether in Drachma, in Euros or in Dollars. (This phenomenon caused the disappearance of silver money from circulation in the world, in the course of the XXth Century).

5. The monetary value which is assigned to the coin shall be slightly higher than the value of the silver contained in the coin. This condition is necessary, to keep the coin in circulation and prevent its being melted down for a higher value in

silver, than its value as Greek money.

6. Whenever the price of silver rises, the Monetary Authority will raise the monetary value of the coin, to a point always slightly higher than the value of the silver contained in the coin.

7. However, if the price of silver falls, the Monetary Authority will retain the last value assigned to the coin. All experience has shown, that a population does not fear falls in the value of silver contained in a silver coin.

8. The population will retain these coins as savings; these will not be susceptible to deposit in the banking system; there will be no "Silver Owl" bank accounts.

9. The banks may establish "Custody Accounts" for the public who wishes to store their "Owls" in a safe place. This will be a storage service, and the coins will remain the property of the owner of a Custody Account.

10. The public may carry out payments either in Drachmas or in "Owls" according to their monetary value. Most Greeks will retain "Owls" in savings, and spend their drachmas – "Gresham's Law".

There, in one page, you have the essentials of a formula to revive Greece and the Spirit of Greece.

I also can foresee that the Greek coin, the "Owl", of 1/10 of a Troy ounce of silver, will become much more desirable on the part of Greeks, than any foreign currency. Your government will have no further problems with "Capital Flight", because Greeks will prefer to own "Owls" rather than any other foreign currency. And banks will have no need to offer high interest rates to attract savings; the silver coin will be so desirable that people will save it simply for its superior quality and future rise in value.

Nor will the Greeks be the only ones to wish to own "Owls"; all of Europe, which uses no silver, will want them. Thus Greece will receive Capital from Europe, for the purchase of "Owls": the purchase of silver is subject to taxation, but the purchase of silver coins that are money is tax-free. (Note as of March 17, 2015: The Greek Government may opt to receive silver objects from individuals, to be returned to them in the form of "Owls". Thus assisting the economic recovery.)

Mr. Tsipras: Can you imagine the power that this new joy and pride in being Greek and having such a superior money, will bring to your government?

As you can see, we are here not talking about "economics", we are talking about the fundamental levers that motivate human beings, levers that have always and everywhere produced great deeds in past ages, and that we, humans of this age, have forgotten while absorbed in electronic fantasies.

I have here outlined the bases to introduce a silver coin that may circulate in parallel with the Drachma.

I have attempted to convince you that this is a plan that you can follow, on your road to greatness as a Statesman who re-established prosperity and joy in his country.

Because China anticipates future problems with the dollar, this letter, in short, illustrates why the Chinese government is presently buying as much gold bullion as it possibly can. It recognizes that gold may one day be the solution to the problem of a new financial system (involving gold-backed currency or trade) that replaces the decaying dollar. Even if it doesn't, gold is still inclined to go up in price if there is a dollar crisis so Chinese gold investments are a win-win any way they look at them.

A harsh reality is that due to strategic mismanagement by western powers the shift in money and financial power has moved eastwards towards China. Eastern nations have established universities and learning institutions on par with the West. They have developed advanced factories and manufacturing facilities that now rival those of the western developed nations. The East offers untapped virgin markets for goods and services while the developed western nations are usually just weaker replacement markets for items like refrigerators, air conditions, televisions and appliances. Strong economic growth is in the East, which is developing a stratum of higher income professionals who can afford to consume.

Most of all, money has been flowing eastward for the products it sends westward. While the rest of the world collects dollars, many eastern nations have been turning their dollar surpluses into gold and silver as insurance against the fact that one day the dollar debt bubble will pop and that currency may become worthless. China and Russia have therefore been accumulating gold bullion not just to prepare for the end of the dollar in trade but as insurance against its default and as preparation for a gold-based system. The U.S. has been doing its best to prevent the inevitable but due to policy blunders the death of the dollar is now virtually certain. The U.S. has made every mistake possible to insure its demise. Will gold take over?

On a net basis a growing number of countries have already been shedding themselves of dollars, sensing its toxic decline, and those numbers are growing. They have been lightening up on U.S. government bond reserves (the vehicle they park their dollars in) with the largest sellers being China, Japan and Saudi Arabia, all of which have traditionally been our largest financiers.

Who then is busy buying all our U.S. Treasury bonds as they are being dumped? Since it is not the typical lenders it must be the ESF through various secretive means using counterparty arrangements that hide the true savior. To prevent failed bond auctions (and thus higher interest rates) the U.S. is actually buying up its own debt using proxies like the ESF for the U.S. Treasury which sets up fake accounts in countries like Belgium, the Bahamas and Ireland to make it appear otherwise.

Can this really be happening? The Bank of England recently admitted that 103 years ago no one was buying British bonds for World War I, so the *Financial Times* went and lied to the public saying that they were oversubscribed. Britain's central bank bought the outstanding securities being offered but covered its tracks by purchasing them under a different name and listing them on its balance sheet as "other securities." The purpose of the lie, it only recently revealed, was to preserve confidence in a fragile system. It was to mislead the public into thinking that the financial position of the British nation was stronger than it actually was. So do governments lie about such things? Yes.

The ESF has exactly the same mandate as the Bank of England had. It is charged with the national security function of maintaining the dollar as the world's reserve currency and global trade payments vehicle, so it is no doubt using all its powers to maintain confidence in the dollar to carry out its primary mandate and thwart the popularity of gold. The challenge, however, is that the problem is now too advanced and severe.

Let's look at a competitor making inroads against the dollar. The Chinese currency accounts for less than 10% of world trade, but China has already made multilateral trade deals that eliminate need for dollar payments with many nations, thus chipping away at the need for countries to hold greenbacks.

Russia is also doing its own part to shed its dollar dependency as well. It has actually made it a priority to cut any dependence on US dollar payment systems. As part of its de-dollarization trend Russia has also become totally free of foreign debt. Furthermore, it is working hard at creating a crude oil and natural gas supply network priced outside the dollar, which would also help break the global monopoly that the US dollar has for energy payments across the world. These moves are all direct challenges to the global hegemony of dollar-based Washington. Let's look at it another way to see if other factors are at play too.

Geopolitically speaking, Russia has extensive untapped natural resources that the West covets while China has the capability to turn them into finished products. These two nations have decided to cooperate with one another. Together the two nations want to create a trading bloc that gets away from the dollar. They are working towards that end, which is why both are periodically demonized by the West. The West cannot attack them militarily and win so it must publicly criticize and condemn them instead.

The Chinese and Russians are simply acting in their own best interests, which is what every nation does, and the West demonizes them because it does not want to see any power or influence escaping its clutches. While the West currently dominates the banking system in the world, we can say that Asia is fast dominating the manufacturing or commercial sector of the world, which is worrying the western nations. Soon the entire world energy markets may be won by the East simply because China doesn't want to buy oil in a currency it does not control.

Right now there is an undeniable attack against the US dollar to reduce its importance in world trade. A big push against the dollar has begun that includes even the electronic rebellion of cryptocurrencies. Many countries are also resorting to some degree of barter trade and starting to experiment with other alternative trading vehicles too. The mistake the U.S. made that got us to this point was to continually abuse its reserve currency status in ever increasing increments, engage in rogue wars everywhere and to finally engage in the hypermonetary printing of debt and currency. Now other countries are seeking safety in other financial vehicles that are not under U.S. control. They are also seeking protection against the fact that the U.S. uses dollar payment mechanisms to impose sanctions on other countries, destabilizing them, and threatens them with exclusion from the payments clearing system. Russia and China are particularly worried about this and therefore making moves to protect themselves. Through abuse of the dollar, Washington has therefore accelerated the destruction of American power abroad.

In short, confidence in both the dollar and the world monetary system is failing. Many mistakes together now threaten the standing of the dollar in trade payments and its reserve currency status.

The Chinese, as students of history, firmly believe that one day the U.S. is probably going to default on its debt through the road of money printed inflation and currency debasement. The Chinese believe this since that is already the road that the U.S. has embarked upon with earnest and which most nations have historically taken. They therefore suspect that U.S. Treasury bond and Treasury bill paper will eventually become worthless somehow, and that their holdings of those debt instruments will collapse when that happens. Like many other nations, in their minds they actually view U.S. Treasury debt as sub-prime and want to get rid of as much as possible. They also want to hedge themselves in case a decline unexpectedly appears and they don't have enough time to race to the exits.

Although the Chinese hold too much U.S. debt to get rid of it entirely they have developed various ways of quietly chipping away at the mountain that don't attract much attention. The Chinese also know that if their central bank stocks up on gold, which will outlast the dollar by preserving value, the renminbi may be one of the few surviving currencies left after a default because that gold will maintain its value, or even become yet more valuable, and will help protect the country's finances.

Holding gold and silver will position the Chinese to make a fortune if the dollar ever collapses. They would be the last man standing with most marbles at the end, readily able to buy up assets on the cheap everywhere while everyone else is eviscerated. They could then claim uncontested wealth and world financial dominance all because western powers tried to deny true reality and were sleeping at the wheel.

Therefore at present the Chinese are actively accumulating incredibly large quantities of gold, which is an undisputed fact. The government does not allow any gold mined within China, for instance, to ever leave the country. China is also importing staggering quantities of bullion through Hong Kong - as much bullion as it possibly can. The Chinese government is even encouraging its citizens to buy physical gold so that more and more of it is pulled into the country.

Remember that the Chinese do not want to destroy the dollar since that would also destroy the world financial system and their own ability to survive. That road of destruction benefits no one, least of all the Chinese who own substantial dollar assets within America and across the world. They are not in a rush to do anything rash and also don't want any blame. They certainly don't want anyone dumping dollars and creating a cascade failure landslide faster than they can hedge against. Nevertheless, they do want to reduce the predominance of the US dollar so that they can benefit.

To help insure any potential transition to a non-dollar based system, China has even started creating modern alternatives to the world financial controlling mechanism previously set up and controlled by the U.S. (the IMF and World Bank). It has set up its own global financial institutions – the Asian Infrastructure Investment Bank and New Development Bank of BRICS - which have dozens of international subscribers. Nearly everyone is on board except the United States since these institutions effectively reduce its influence.

Even though China is pushing to decrease the international dependence on the dollar, the renminbi itself cannot become the new world reserve currency. The reason is because Chinese business doesn't amount to enough of world trade nor does China have enough debt instruments in which other countries can park their idle funds. Therefore China must turn to a liquid, internationally traded vehicle, such as gold, to replace dollar dependency. Turning to gold bypasses all concerns about China and brings about trust in a strong dollar alternative. The best alternative is therefore a return to the *historically proven* gold standard that once presided over the longest stretch of prosperity in U.S. history with very little inflation. China and Russia are therefore now building out new gold systems not controlled by the West.

No single nation, or even group of just a few nations, can succeed in setting up the gold standard by themselves. As soon as a single country instituted a gold standard for its currency, other nations would buy that currency and consequently bid up its price, thus making its exports unaffordable and killing its economy. A large number of countries would therefore have to simultaneously switch over to the new system in order that a majority of world trade could safely be affected at the same time. Otherwise the feedback forces would be too great to absorb if countries too few in number tried to do this prematurely.

A critical mass of countries must reach a consensus and be willing to simultaneously switch over at the same time, which is exactly what the rallying around the Eurasian Trade Zone is attempting to achieve. The Eurasian Trade Zone and New Silk Road are not only development efforts to fuel economies for decades but a way to gather nations together toward participation in a new monetary system no longer dependent on the US dollar. The partners of the Shanghai Cooperative Organization (SCO), which represents a population of over 3 billion people (42% of world population), are also coming together in a coherent, cohesive cooperation that is pursuing the architecture of a new monetary alternative to the US dollar. The countries involved in China's One Belt, One Road initiative amount to an even greater 62% of the world's population, over half of its GDP and 75% of its hydrocarbon resources too.

As you know, various forces are currently building non-USD platforms and market mechanisms that will serve the New Silk Road. The New Silk Road infrastructure projects will involve non-USD international projects on a grand scale. The U.S. is trying to thwart and delay such attempts, but will lose in the end because the demand for alternatives is now too great because of prior American abuses. Even so, the U.S. will try to obstruct any attempts at creating US dollar alternatives, and will wage a virtual jihad against any county, company or individual who tries to create gold-based monetary instruments since they threaten the dollar.

Strategically speaking, is this not the right course of action? Strategically speaking again, since decline seems inevitable, should not the U.S. be preparing for a new system, or at least hedging its potential risks, by buying lots more gold? If a gold system is not guaranteed but only likely, once again shouldn't the U.S. government start quietly amassing more precious metals? Yes, because the Petrodollar system is seeing its last legs.

Although the U.S. traditionally dominates in the field of war (which is actually its most powerful "financial weapon"), other than the ESF and its activities it does not have as many offensive and defensive mechanisms in the financial arena. Of course the U.S. can also enforce trade sanctions against countries and curtail money flows by tampering with the SWIFT system that transmits financial transactions data across the world (between 10,500 large financial institutions in 215 countries). For instance, SWIFT de-listed 30 Iranian financial institutions in 2012 while the idea of delisting Russian banks was also floated at a later time when tensions rose between a U.S. bloc of nations and Russia.

This is exactly why China and Russia have been hard at work setting up an alternative trade payments infrastructure of their own, just in case at some point in time the "completely independent" SWIFT organization is used as a proxy weapon against them by the U.S. State Department. Knowing that it had to free itself from transactions-related risks so that the U.S. had no leverage over it, China has created its own alternative to SWIFT called CIPS (Cross-Border Inter-Bank Payment System) while Russia has launched its own SWIFT-alternative too. These are further evidence that the power of King Dollar is waning.

If the U.S. ever tries to impose monetary sanctions by use of SWIFT, these countries and others using the new Eurasian systems will now be immune because of these new safe havens. Russia is in even better condition than China in terms of financial protection since it has virtually no foreign debt and plenty of food and energy resources that other countries need. Together with Russia, China is building alternative payment channels and exchanges wherever necessary to replace any reliance on the dollar and is actually the center of the worldwide "resistance bloc" to the status quo.

In terms of attempts to bypass US dollar trade and the Petrodollar standard, President Putin of Russia also recently made the public statement, "Russia shares the BRICS countries' concerns over the unfairness of the global financial and economic architecture, which does not give due regard to the growing weight of the emerging economies. We are ready to work together with our partners to promote international financial regulation reforms and to overcome the excessive domination of the limited number of reserve currencies." Funny enough, the United Nations even said we need "a new global reserve system … that no longer relies on the United States dollar as the single major reserve currency."

The installation of the gold standard, if it happens, will reset the entire world financial system because it would decrease the power of the dollar and also restrict the powers of governments to print money at will without consequence. A gold trade system will basically redefine the role for the western central banking system, pushing many entities out of their current positions of power and control. Resistance against it therefore will be strong, so it will most likely be ushered in only under adverse conditions such as the present system's failure.

When President Nixon took the U.S. off the gold standard in 1971 the value of the U.S. dollar then became independent of gold and totally dependent on its prudent management by the Federal Reserve. The country was told that the Federal Reserve would thereafter be able to use its extensive powers to bring prosperity to America. It was promised that the Fed's powers to manipulate the monetary system free of the gold standard would produce strong economic growth, provide high employment, reduce the U.S. trade deficit, improve the competitiveness of American workers and avoid recessions. What a failure since every promise has been broken!

We are presently in a situation, derived from a long sequence of events, where millions of Americans have now lost full time employment with benefits due to jobs being offshored. They have been forced into lower wage part time and contract employment that leaves them with little discretionary income after payment of their health insurance, medical debt, credit card debt, automobile debt, student loan debt, or mortgage interest and fees. If they go broke they will lose most of these things and then have a lower standard of living. On top of these payments and bad jobs in a consumer-based economy thriving on debt, they are on the hook for bailing out financial institutions that made foolish and risky investments. Additionally, debt has run amuck.

What will a gold standard do? A gold standard will stabilize prices while eliminating the destructive forces inherent within a zero percent interest rate economy. A more stable economy will lead to more stable growth without inflation, and a chance for competitive jobs to be born again. A gold standard will turn the current power structure upside down across the world because it is the arch-enemy of the system of catering to the big banks and printing money whenever the government wants. It will prevent the overprinting of money to bail out big banks and the printing of money to cover federal deficits.

Gold is the arbiter of fairness and equitability because it forces a just system of worldwide equilibrium. It even prevents war because military excursions require extreme money printing and debt levels that would, under a gold standard, crush a nation's currency. For instance, countries were forced to go off the gold standard so that they could print sufficient money to wage WWI. A gold standard imposes the discipline of putting military spending and war in check while putting industry and trade at the forefront of domestic concerns.

Because it imposes financial discipline on a nation, a gold standard will establish a solid foundation for future economic growth. It will create a stable world financial system once again, but not without an enormously staggering period of disruption as the old system is replaced. For instance, under a gold standard the nations which sport large trade deficits will face the prospect of losing national assets to pay for their trade imbalances. Thus they will suffer a shock wave of rapid change when they are forced to embark upon national initiatives to export more to reduce possible deficits. Exports will be emphasized in the extreme. Those countries will have to invite in more foreign capital investment and clear the way for more domestic business formation.

Historically speaking, whenever a reserve currency is

transitioned over to a new one the world faces a period of financial instability, uncertainty, and turmoil. China holds enormous quantities of U.S. debt so it does not want a rapid default on its holdings because of instabilities. It wants to wash its hands of the dollar by lowering its dependence on the currency, but what will happen to the dollar if its deterioration proceeds too fast? If the dollar's value collapses like a rock falling off a cliff then so will the value of any Chinese held dollar-denominated assets. You don't want a situation where all the countries of the world are simultaneously rushing to the exits because that will utterly collapse the U.S. markets. China and Russia definitely want to build a parallel system for the dollar's replacement so the infrastructure is slowly being developed and evolved into place. They expect the US dollar system to break down on its own and don't want to be labeled the "bad guy" who did it.

If there is to be an orderly transition to a new prosperity that is not based on the dollar, the global economic system must be put on life support during any transition period. A colossal amount of infrastructure construction projects and new business must be initiated to buffer the shocks. Doing so will put people back to work, but more importantly, in a constructive manner. China plans to do this through a trillion dollar set of infrastructure projects shifting towards the Eurasian trade zone and its One Belt One Road initiative. This will weave together a vast new market that will far overshadow any future potentials in the debt-bloated markets of the western OECD countries. What is the United States doing? Not much.

Famed analyst Jim Willie has surmised that gold will return to the world's monetary systems first in the trade finance arena as gold trade note letters of credit. This will be a new system of net trade settlement in gold, which will then cause gold to enter into the banking system, and finally gold-backed currencies will develop. He surmises that gold will first be installed in trade payments first, then banking reserves, and finally in currency backing.

What might a future gold trade note used for trade payment look like? The gold trade notes that could eventually lead to a gold standard might initially be commodity transfers, later swap contracts, and finally gold-backed short-term notes. These notes would replace the U.S. Treasury bill, which is the short-term debt instrument currently dominating international trade.

Who would likely introduce the gold trade note? The Chinese are already in the midst of a de-dollarization move. Some day China will probably encourage all the Eurasian trade participants and members of the One Belt One Road initiative to use the gold trade note rather than U.S. Treasury notes or Treasury bills. Then international trade would be conducted in gold trade notes, a short-term note backed by gold rather than U.S. debt. Moving in that direction, China just introduced a crude oil futures contract denominated in renminbi (yuan) and convertible into gold. This one step in itself may directly lead to the death of the Petrodollar, which is truly unraveling, and the birth of the gold trade note in short order.

When oil is not universally paid for in dollars anymore it will be like opening a can of worms where anything can pop out. If a gold-backed replacement for trade then takes hold it will knock the dollar dead in the trade payments arena. Countries would then reduce their dollar exposure in their banking systems and eventually gold-backed currencies will arise. The death of Petrodollar within all this will surely set off military conflicts, none of which will be in the interests of the United States. What we need now are leaders who will systematically think out policies for the coming economic and financial tsunami.

What can you and should you do to protect yourself? Buy physical gold and silver, hold them outside of the banking system by storing them safely in another country or domestically out of the reach of the government.

8
GOLD INVESTMENTS AS YOUR INSURANCE SHIELD

Do you remember the American Express commercial that went, "When it absolutely, positively has to be there overnight"? In terms of the safety of your financial assets, there are absolutely, positively good reasons for you to have some physical gold and silver bullion in your wealth portfolio. With the forces now threatening the dollar, rather than holding 100% of your wealth in paper assets a portion should reside in precious metals. Even the cryptocurrencies are not as secure because if the electricity goes out they are killed in one instant.

The first principle to recognize when considering gold and silver investments is that they are a form of savings and insurance rather than an ordinary speculative play. In other words, you should not buy gold and silver to trade them. They are meant to help you preserve your wealth in a financial world gone wild. You should consider them as a form of wealth insurance or protection rather than just a trade.

Historically speaking, precious metal investments are a

savings mechanism that has been used for thousands of years, outlasting every world currency! You must therefore think of gold and silver as a long-term means to protect your wealth regardless of the fate of paper currencies.

There have been many difficult times in history when protecting your wealth has become more important than trying to earn a return on that wealth. Our present era of zero interest rates due to QE money printing is one of those times when you should be more concerned with the risks overshadowing the safety of your assets rather than the possible yield on those assets.

Mark Twain once jokingly stated, "I am more concerned about the return of my money than the return on my money," and this quip summarizes the dangers in today's environment. We are living in a financial world reminiscent of a Ponzi scheme because central banks are so indebted that they are printing money to cover the financing of their own interest rate debt. They must also keep interest rates low to reduce their own financial burdens, and some countries (U.S., Japan, etc.) are even buying their own debt because no one else will. They are doing so in order to save their financial systems and that need to save their own systems means that *your own assets are someway at risk.*

This is something you must deeply consider, especially in light of the fact that many analysts believe we have entered the "endgame" for fiat paper currencies, the supremacy of the US dollar in global trade, and unchecked central bank money-printing policies. All these possibilities suggest potential future chaos in the financial markets for which we should buy some type of protective insurance.

Because world central banks are in a historically unprecedented state of grand-scale collusion and printing massive quantities of money while keeping interest rates low in order to prevent massive debt defaults, the present times are now matching historical situations where similar policies led to financial destruction. The only people who have benefited from these actions are the big banks who have profited from the access to cheap money. Bankism has enriched them tremendously.

During previous periods of unlimited government spending, money printing and debts, people preserved their wealth by investing in safer stores of value other than paper assets. The safest alternatives have always been the precious metals.

Now why are the precious metals considered a safer way to store your wealth than a fiat currency? The answer, as previously explained, is because they are internationally traded assets with no counterparty risks. Their prices will never go to zero so they can always serve as a stable medium of exchange. They even tend to increase in price during financial crises because they represent insurance *and* a store of value that embodies other beneficial characteristics.

All debt that exists carries a risk that the counterparty issuing it won't pay back what's owed. Even government currency has a risk that the paper may not retain its value over time, which is why people in economically weak countries usually protect their wealth by holding traditionally stronger currencies like the US dollar, Euro and Swiss Franc. The Zimbabwean dollar, for instance, has suffered such massive hyperinflation that the currency is now virtually worthless. It even includes 100 trillion dollar notes. Hyperinflation is happening in Venezuela and also rendering its currency worthless, even though both these currencies are "backed by tax receipts" and the "full faith and credit of the government." The value of currencies can indeed go to zero, which is why smart people turn to gold and silver to preserve a portion of their financial assets. Inflation or hyperinflation are just two of the many risks that might destroy the value of a currency.

Whenever an entity goes bankrupt then any debt it owes decreases in value. When that happens for a country most of its paper assets, such as stocks and bonds, will also see lower prices. While tangible real assets that produce income - such as farmland, oil wells, timber, mines, etc. – also carry these risks to some extent, the fact that they can independently throw off income even during bad financial times tends to make them valuable during severe crises that become survival emergencies.

The point is that when you want to preserve wealth in a fragile financial system or during shaky financial times, you need to invest some money in assets that will retain their values better than everything else, and which also have no counterparty claims on them so that they cannot be taken away. Precious metals fit this bill nicely and are one of the safest ways to store your wealth for all sorts of adverse financial conditions.

No one knows how high gold and silver prices can ultimately go during the next global financial crisis, so we cannot bank on forecasts to guide investment decisions in the precious metals. Instead we must refer back to an understanding of history to help guide our decisions. Nonetheless, because it is of such great interest we would like to share some price possibilities put forth by top analysts who have studied the matter deeply and - using various forms of historical analysis and calculations - have come to some conclusions.

Super gold analyst Jim Willie once said it will probably hit $7,000 per ounce and may go to $15,000 per ounce or more. Jim Rickards, author of *Currency Wars* and *The Death of Money*, thinks that the price of gold may go to $7,000 or $9,000 per ounce because he believes that the dollar may be devalued by 80% or 90% for reasons already discussed. Famous gold trader, James Sinclair, believes that gold may go to $50,000 per ounce, in gradual steps, because of the collapse of the US dollar and the fiat currency system.

No one knows for sure what gold's ultimate price trajectory will be if we encounter a worldwide crisis due to a loss of confidence in fiat currencies because of the excessive money printing of central banks. One should follow Warren Buffett's principle of never trusting in forecasts and predictions, which I emphasized in my book *Super Investing*, but instead rely on basic investment principles and historical analysis. Even so, the bottom line is that people wishing to protect themselves should probably hold some gold and silver in their portfolios as insurance against the demise of the dollar and possible restructuring of the world's financial system. The little price you pay for buying financial insurance, by investing in the precious metals, may one day seem just a fraction of the money you save through such action.

One day the suppression of the gold price to eliminate dollar competition will no longer be possible because its physical price will be emancipated from the manipulated price of the paper futures markets. Central bankers or their agents currently enter the paper futures market during the thinnest trading hours of the day and then dump (sell) on the market great quantities of gold contracts - equivalent to many months worth of gold production - simply to drive prices down to protect the dollar. A declining dollar price of gold makes the dollar look strong. If gold prices are kept down, people are less likely to consider gold as an alternative to the dollar.

This manipulation is unmistakable, yet is permitted to continue because it is used as a tool to help protect the dollar's value. Soon, however, it may be gone. The ability to paper short the market may be curtailed because new exchanges are arising that will trade the actual physical metals on a 24-hour basis and curtail naked shorting. The physical exchanges require actual inventories of gold and silver that cannot just be printed into existence out of thin air.

China and many other nations have been accumulating gold at rock bottom prices when the paper prices are manipulated downwards, profiting from this manipulated stupidity of the central bankers. Unfortunately for bullion banks they have been emptying their vaults trying to satisfy the demand for physical deliveries at the lower prices. Their own inventories have almost been emptied. There is actually a very real shortage in the marketplace for physical gold. All the gold is going from the west to the east, from weak hands to stronger hands, just as financial power is draining away from the USA and Europe and also heading to Asia.

Previously any banks buying gold usually kept it in the London pool, but now China is buying it and asking for physical delivery, thus draining it from the western system. As it accumulates more gold its political power actually increases. The physical market is becoming strained from purchases, but the paper market is one hundred times larger, which is why the financial institutions are using it to push gold prices downwards to save the dollar. When the market eventually sees there is no gold to deliver against the paper longs (the bullion banks won't be able to deliver on the paper) then cash settlement will occur instead, and the paper manipulation will cease.

This is not what central banks or bullion banks want, but the more they push down prices the higher the physical demand becomes for gold and silver due to the risks that everyone now knows permeates the global financial system. Because of artificially suppressed bargain basement prices while financial instabilities rise, the demand for physical gold bullion has become insatiable since wise individuals and countries see gold accumulation as a measure of prudence. Some people see buying some Bitcoin a prudent measure as well even though no one even knows if the cryptocurrency will exist in the future. Governments might be able to regulate or tax it out of existence, or eventually penetrate its walls of privacy that make it attractive.

What is most probable in my view is that governments want to withdraw banknotes from circulation and issue digital fiat currency similar to cryptocurrency. Then governments will be able to monitor and control all the transactions within an economy by using digital fiat as a tool of control. If you don't have the right government-issued licenses or it simply doesn't "like you" then the government could then lock you out of the payments system. Bitcoin gives you a way to escape all of this. It gives you the capability to store money in a currency other than your own (the international value of Bitcoin) and transfer money without interference restrictions from the government. Bitcoin helps you hedge your exposure to any economic meltdown possible in your country. Being "long crypto" is actually a way to "hedge against government" since it gives you an international storage and transactions vehicle that is private and secure. This is the function that gold and silver as *real goods* have performed for centuries.

If the blockchain technology of cryptocurrencies is ever hooked up to the ownership of gold and silver, then hop on board because this will be the game changer that will free those markets from the last vestiges of price manipulation. Tangible assets are starting to migrate to the blockchain technology of cryptocurrencies and this will slowly put manipulated markets and various avenues of deep state funding out of business. This is because blockchain technology brings honesty and integrity to the transmission and ownership of tangible things. Exchanges built upon fraudulent paper practices cannot survive such an assault.

The day will eventually come when the LBME and Comex exchanges for precious metals will not be able to deliver any more physical gold and silver to meet the demand for physical deliveries. At that time the exchanges will have to make contract changes to avoid default, and then settle the paper futures contracts in cash. At that time the physical market will finally be emancipated from the futures markets.

When that happens, you will suddenly see jumps of $100 or $200 per day in the prices of the precious metals. At that time, any physical forms of gold and silver will become hard to find, and that future scarcity is another reason to buy ahead of time and store them away for your wealth portfolio.

Analyst Alasdair Macleod has wisely stated, "At some stage China with her SCO partner, Russia, will force the price of gold higher as part of their currency strategy. You can argue this from an economic point of view on the basis that possession of properly priced gold will give her a financial dominance over global trade at a time when we are trashing our fiat currencies, or more simply that there is no point in owning an asset and suppressing its value forever."

Although you should probably accumulate gold and silver to protect yourself when the era of Bankism goes bust, you should not focus on becoming a gold and silver trader. You can certainly trade these markets but the emphasis should be on holding the precious metals as a long-term investment.

Gold expert Jim Sinclair warns that in trying to trade gold you are up against some of the smartest minds in the world who have incredibly deep pockets. He has stated that gold trading on the Comex and LBME exchanges is an insider's game of a manipulated market, and you are not an insider so are doomed to fail in this trading game. Since you therefore cannot compete, your best option is simply to buy physical gold and silver and hold it rather than trade it. Holding physical gold and silver is your insurance policy whereas trading gold and silver is not the road to wealth.

If you are going to buy gold and silver, the best advice is that you should buy physical bullion, bars and/or coins and always take delivery of the metals. You should never use margin to buy either. It is also imperative that you never store your holdings at a bank but always safely store them outside of the banking system simply because banks (and the government) cannot be trusted during financial crises. If the cryptocurrency blockchain technology is ever married with the buying and selling of gold and silver, then this will bring integrity to the precious metals market allowing even safer methods of ownership and storage.

How much do experts recommend you buy of gold and silver?

Once again the answer is not cut and dry, but a general rule of thumb that analysts bandy about is between 10% and 30% of your portfolio. Dr. Marc Faber recently suggested a 25% allocation to precious metals. Back when I worked for Wall Street in the 80s, I ran dozens of computer studies to determine the best composition of a buy-and-hold wealth portfolio consisting of stocks, bonds, foreign currencies, commodities and physical gold. At that time I found that allocating 10-20% of one's assets to gold was the optimal amount to help protect and grow such a fund over the long run.

Recently I heard an interview with another analyst who, running more current computer studies entirely different from my own, also found that devoting 20% of one's portfolio to precious metals produced the best reward/risk performance in the long run. You should therefore think of possible allocations in terms of units such as 5%, 10%, 15%, 20% or 25%.

How much one invests in gold and silver, and in what form, depends on how concerned you are about the current economic, financial and political situation of your country and the world. All in all, everyone should probably buy some physical gold and silver for their portfolio to protect themselves. The precious metals are a form of protective insurance against wealth destruction. Individuals should also hold them in some private way that is outside of the manipulative reach of the banking system.

It is difficult to determine the best forms of gold and/or silver to buy because everyone's situation is different. Some forms will be more liquid or popular in different areas of the world. Some will be less risky, better suited for international diversification, or will outperform others if there is a sharp run-up in precious metals prices.

Some are easier/cheaper to buy or sell, less likely to be targeted in a confiscation, or easier to store. Some will offer greater purchasing power protection than others. Even though there are so many possibilities, your best choices basically come down to bullion, bars and coins.

If you want to buy gold and silver coins, you should stay away from exotic coins or rarities. You should consider buying bullion coins rather than numismatic coins. Collecting numismatic coins should primarily be for fun, not profit, because they always cost you both a numismatic premium and a dealer's spread above the cost of the underlying metal. Furthermore, if you buy and then immediately try to sell a numismatic coin you are likely to lose between 30-50% of your investment, which is also something to consider. For investments you should rely on highly liquid, easily traded bullion coins or bars that are portable and easy to store.

For gold bullion coins, the most popular coin varies widely among world regions. The most popular gold coin in the U.S. is the Gold Eagle while the most popular gold coin in Canada is the Gold Maple Leaf. The most popular gold coin in Europe is the Gold Austrian Philharmonic. China also issues the Gold Chinese Panda, South Africa issues the Krugerrand, and Australia issues the Gold Australian Kangaroo. These are the major gold coins to consider.

As regards silver bullion coins your most popular options are American Silver Eagles, Canadian Silver Maple Leafs, the Silver Austrian Philharmonic, the Silver Mexican Libertad and various Australian silver coins issued by the Perth Mint.

For gold and silver bars and rounds the options are even wider in scope. To buy bullion coins or bars there are a number of highly reputable dealers that you can easily find on the internet such as SDBullion.com, Silver.com, Metals.com, and others. Always search around for whomever will provide bullion bars or coins at the lowest premium over the spot price of gold and silver. Usually I've found that SDBullion.com or Metals.com wins this race.

If you want to diversify your bullion holdings and also buy precious metals stocks, there are two types to consider.

First, there are stocks that are trusts holding actual physical bullion, like the Sprott PHYS and PSLV funds or the CES Central Fund of Canada that holds mixed quantities of gold and silver bullion. If you want to be holding physical bullion through stocks then PHYS, PSLV and CES fit the bill. Hard asset experts consistently give these three funds top marks because they are well managed and audits always show that the physical gold or silver is actually there.

That is not the case with 90% of the "paper gold" products out there in the marketplace. Warnings are constantly issued along these lines about GLD and SLV because while they are good for liquid trading purposes, at the end of the day they are still just paper promises for owning precious metals. Paper promises are no replacement for holding the real asset. You want to be holding the actual metals themselves rather than pieces of paper which say some entity is holding metals for you though they might not actually be doing so.

There are also precious metals mining company shares for investment that are basically leveraged plays on the price of gold and silver. This is not a preferred form of investing over actual bullion holdings because picking the best gold and silver mining stocks requires a lot of analysis involving many tangled issues.

One of the potential dangers in mining shares is that those firms and their properties might be one day coveted by governments, or even become subject to massive windfall taxes if the price of gold and silver should ever skyrocket. If those properties are in foreign jurisdictions, there is little you can do about this. This once again suggests that your "safety," "insurance" or "wealth protection" holdings of precious metals should primarily consist of readily tradable bullion bars and coins that you actually physically hold.

If you are going to buy bullion yourself, such as silver and gold coins and bullion bars, you'll need to store them. You can do that at home or by using a storage facility. Quite a few hard asset advocates stress that you should avoid the precious metals storage vaults located in the western banking system, especially those located in New York, London and Switzerland.

For instance, gold expert Egon von Greyerz have reported that wealthy families have stored their gold in allocated Swiss accounts for years, but many who asked for delivery have recently been told that their Swiss bank could not and would not supply the gold it was supposed to be holding. Fishy things have been going on in Switzerland in regards to "allocated" gold accounts, but any lawsuits related to these matters are quietly kept out of the press because of the potential damage to the Swiss banking system.

Neither London nor the U.S. banks have spotless reputations as regards managing allocated or "segregated" bullion accounts either. In many cases, in these locations it is also possible that your allocated bullion has been loaned out to other parties and is not sitting in the vaults that you are paying storage on each month. In other words, clients have been told their gold is sitting in the bank's vaults and they are being charged storage fees, but their gold isn't actually there. It was "loaned out" to another party who doubtless sold it in the market, but who paid an interest fee to the bank for the "loan." If that has happened to your account and you ask for your gold back, you may never see it. To protect yourself you should try to transfer it out and take possession of it *now*.

You should always try to store your gold outside the banking system. History has shown countless instances where the government and large banking entities will suddenly change their rules in such a way that the changes could harm you and your money. In the future such events might even include the confiscation of whatever precious metals you have in the financial system if larger entities feel they can easily get their hands on it.

Always, always remember that in addition to buying from reputable dealers, you should store any precious metals where no government can get its hands on them because of the simple rule that "what governments cannot find they cannot confiscate." This is why many people choose to store their gold and silver investments in offshore private vaults that are outside of domestic banking influences.

If you want to select a bullion storage provider, here are the due diligence concerns that you should always consider:

- Make sure that your bullion storage provider and sourcing provider both have adequate insurance cover.
- Make sure that your bullion is being sourced from recognized refiners known for their integrity such as those within the LBMA chain (so that when you buy bullion you can be 100% sure it is actually physical bullion).
- Never choose paper, pooled or digital bullion, and only choose fully allocated bullion accounts that also offer segregated storage of your precious metals.
- Make sure that your provider conducts regular audits, using internationally recognized auditors, and that owner-directed audits are available on demand while standard audits are done according to a regular schedule.

- Make sure that you can take delivery of your bullion, including the ability to have it shipped to you.
- Make sure that you can keep track of your bullion holdings online, including being able to review the weight, quantity, fineness, purchase costs and dates and other characteristics of your holdings.
- Make sure that you can visit your provider and actually view your bullion holdings (whether physical coins or bars).
- Make sure that the true ownership of your bullion always remains with you rather than that the provider or any other party holds it in your name (while you store it with someone else you must still own it and have real control over it).
- Make sure that your provider can facilitate the sale of your bullion, when you want, in a timely, efficient and expedited manner so that you can turn it into cash whenever you desire.

Remember that some gold storage companies may entice you by offering ultra cheap storage, sometimes below the actual vaulting costs for the precious metals. Why would anyone do that? Only if the low storage fees you are being charged are subsidized by some other revenue stream. A subsidy from other possible revenue streams (such as interest on currency deposits or speculation profits) suggests that your bullion may be at risk, so be careful with ultra cheap storage facilities.

With all these concerns in mind, individuals should look to reputable companies for coin and bullion purchases, and for storage facilities that will hold your bullion outside of the banking system. Three such entities that are commonly cited for physical bullion purchase and storage include:

- GoldMoney.com – founded by James Turk
- GoldSwitzerland.com – Egon von Greyerz
- SGPMX.com - Singapore gold exchange

All in all, using gold and silver investing as a form of insurance against the excesses of Bankism is a lengthy topic involving many hows, whys and wherefores. The short recap of the history for you to consider in protecting yourself, and for analyzing whether you should become a buyer, is as follows.

All fiat currencies eventually collapse. Therefore that will also eventually be the same fate for the US dollar one day. Reserve currencies also change and financial systems are frequently retooled over time too. Nothing is granted the boon of perpetuity. Financial systems eventually collapse from too much debt and excessive money printing, and this cycle has been repeated for thousands of years. Many analysts believe that this will happen to the U.S., and that the death of the dollar is therefore near at hand.

No one knows whether any of this will happen to any of us in the next six months, next year, or in the next decade but macro events in the world definitely suggest that a tipping point may be near at hand for some of these potentials. The tide is moving in this direction, especially due to moves by Russia and China.

Therefore you should consider devoting some portion of your investments to tangible, hard assets simply because they represent wealth insurance against a fragile banking system, toxic debts and the death of the dollar. In today's world real assets represent insurance against the wealth destructive policies of central bankers like the Fed.

Gold and silver are *real tangible assets* that have represented wealth for thousands of years, and they have been shown to be able to hold your purchasing power during difficult times including both deflation and inflation. They have often been a "safe port" whenever there has been a financial storm of monetary messiness. They are a form of wealth preservation. While Bitcoin is also a way to preserve and transfer wealth at the moment, its existence depends upon computer systems and electricity whereas gold and silver do not. The government can also ban Bitcoin and other currencies at any moment, even though they serve as relief valves for monetary inflation, but cannot get rid of physical gold and silver.

The precious metals are real assets that have no counterparty risk (though only if you actually own them free of any encumbrances and hold them yourself by taking delivery) and they can serve as insurance for various types of financial crisis that periodically happen in the world. The fact that various fundamental forces may soon move their prices dramatically upwards is just icing on the cake beyond these basic reasons for holding precious metals in a portfolio. The sound reasons hold regardless of the naysayers.

Right now, old financial systems have reached critical crisis points because of massive amounts of government (and private) debts and are breaking down. Never before have so many major nations run massive government deficits that have created debts in the trillions of dollars. The banking systems of countless nations, undercapitalized in the extreme and full of toxic debt, are also now extremely vulnerable to bankruptcy. No amount of tax dollars can pay off these debts as they are over-leveraged in the extreme. For some countries, even the total wealth of the nation cannot be used to pay off the debts of that country!

International markets are also over-burdened with unfathomably complex SWAP and derivative liabilities connected to this debt or the US dollar that also dwarf the size of world GNP many times over. They represent a potential domino effect of interlinked banking defaults that could collapse the entire world's banking system should one big bank go bad.

At the same time we face all these risks, various countries are quietly moving ahead to reduce the importance of the US dollar in world trade, which is also damaging its role as the global reserve currency. The Petrodollar is at risk. It is failing.

If people lose confidence in the dollar for any reason whatsoever, then because of supply and demand factors the gold and silver markets could skyrocket.

As people liable to lose all of our wealth should something go wrong, we need to understand these current trends as well as the lessons of financial history. You cannot just ignore history and say that fiat currencies will never fail, reserve currencies will never change and financial systems will never have to be retooled. You cannot say that countries will never change their global status of predominance because leaders are constantly being replaced by competitors all the time.

All these things commonly happen and will do so into the future. We cannot say that the time for anything specific to happen is *now*, but we can recognize that you better be prepared with insurance for some high probability calamities that might just happen in today's world financial system. Gold and silver are the means to do so. They can protect against the excesses caused by Bankism that now threaten the financial system and the fate of the US dollar.

At the end of a fiat currency system, countries typically experience one of either two fates: (1) either a deflationary collapse occurs with debt defaults, or (2) an inflationary collapse (hyperinflation) occurs with subsequent currency reform. In both of these possibilities, gold and silver are some of the most important assets you can hold to protect yourself. They enable you to preserve your wealth through the crisis. They also protect your wealth from a government hell-bent on confiscating your money through any means possible.

Gold and silver are highly portable. You can take them

anywhere in the world and they will still hold their value. You can also easily store them away and then exchange them for money, goods or services whenever you need it. Both of these precious metals enable you to store some of your assets in a better way than in a paper currency that is declining in value. Gold and silver coins and bars are therefore one of the best ways to achieve this objective. If history does in fact repeat itself, the cost of this insurance will be tremendously cheap in relation to the wealth it would conserve in the future.

If we enter a period of hyperinflation due to excessive money printing that grows vertically (because we cannot fund our debt obligations yet must still satisfy them by printing money to prevent the system from imploding) then the nominal value of gold and silver will probably go up very much as they went up in the 1970s. A similar situation happened in France during the French Revolution when gold increased 288 times in value in just five years, 1790 to 1795. This is how gold protects you during a time of crisis.

When money printing grows at an unsustainable vertical rate, the infinite rate of increase never makes what is around worth more than what it was worth in earlier times. Thus at some point in our current times, the value of the dollar will have to decline and at that time the precious metals, since they have an independent international pricing, will shine as the best store of value through that process. If crisis strikes, they might experience a shortage so severe that you might not be able to get any from the marketplace at all. Prudence therefore requires one to think about accumulating some now.

CONCLUSION

Most times the people who lost the most money during difficult financial times (such as the retooling of a financial system) were those who did not make provisions to survive the maelstrom. They didn't see anything coming and thus prepare with adequate financial insurance. Why? Because they were trapped within an outdated worldview.

Gold and silver holdings serve as the proper form of insurance for our present era of Bankism gone haywire with its attendant black swan events. As financial stability decreases in the world the faith in precious metals (and cryptocurrencies) will increase. They are insurance against errant financial policies, the follies of international central bankers, and unexpected financial catastrophes caused by a world overstocked with unpayable debts. There should be some gold and silver in your portfolio, and possibly some cryptocurrencies like Bitcoin that can help you get around government attempts to devalue your currency or restrict its movements or conversion into other items of value.

Bitcoin is like a digital bearer instrument that can be used in anonymous transactions, including international payments without fees. It is still in its infancy and so doesn't yet have widespread adoption. Its price is totally determined by the market and no one can predict its future, but its existence can at the present help you store value outside of the US dollar or escape currency controls in a nation. Fiat currencies have value because people place faith in the governments that issue them, and the very same thing actually applies to the value of Bitcoin. So who can say how much it is really worth? Will its value hold in the future, and will it even exist in the future or be outlawed?

No one knows, but prudence suggests that one should set up the ability to buy Bitcoin now before currency controls make it impossible to do so. If a government runs into financial trouble it will certainly try to restrict the conversion of its currency through capital controls, which is what historically happens, and obstruct its transformation into alternative stores of wealth. Bitcoin can help you escape those possible restrictions.

The true value of Bitcoin will only be seen when a

global financial crisis hits the central banks of the world and people react against newly enacted capital controls. To me its best usage is to escape the restrictions of currency controls in a nation, such as in China or Venezuela at present. However, to me the best form of cryptocurrency going forward will not be Bitcoin but gold-backed cryptocurrencies yet to be developed. Gold-backed cryptocurrencies, where your ownership is registered on the blockchain, will prevent ownership fraud because ownership is documented. It will bring integrity to the gold and silver markets whereas this problem plagues the fiat paper games played on the LBME and Comex exchanges. In those paper markets the large banks can sell unlimited quantities of precious metals contracts equating to enormous amounts of precious metals that don't exist, haven't yet been mined and never will be.

Time and again one of the best protections for financial times that shook the fate of nations was to hold the precious metals of gold and silver. This has been one of the few dependable ways to protect and preserve your wealth throughout all sorts of financial crises, and in particular the possible financial changes potentially coming.

Of course, this has always been dependent on the fact that you actually *own* the gold and silver rather than that someone *owes* you gold and silver. If your ownership is not under your complete control, there is always the possibility that the other party might not satisfy its obligations to you during a crisis.

If a bank owes you gold and silver, for instance, that won't do you any good during a crisis if that counterparty bank becomes insolvent or the government changes the laws and tries to confiscate it from the banks. That's why most people try to hold precious metals in their own hands or in some safe location outside the fragile banking system.

Whenever any nation runs into financial troubles, people ordinarily rush to safety by either exchanging their cash for a safer, stronger currency or by buying the precious metals. First, they run from their domestic fiat currency to other currencies because that is the easiest and most familiar option. Typically they try to exchange their own currency for the world's reserve currency since it is usually considered the safest currency around.

For most people this has been the easiest option to financially protect themselves during domestic troubles. *When the reserve currency itself is in financial danger, however, then your next best option is to turn to gold and silver.* They have no debt attached to them and no counterparty risk that they will fail, but they can still readily serve as exchangeable money. They have stood as an emergency store of value for thousands of years.

This is where the value of precious metals shines. *They enable you to store your savings in an alternative, better way than paper currencies during a financial crisis. In difficult times, owning gold and silver often represent the best type of financial insurance, protection and profits. When countries destroy their currencies, gold and silver hold their value through it all.*

Hundreds of fiat currencies in the world have passed away into oblivion, but this has never happened for gold and silver. Fiat paper currencies, reserve currencies and financial systems may come and go, but gold and silver have survived them all. They have been money for thousands of years and you can bet for sure that they will retain their value into the future no matter what happens to King Dollar.

Gold and silver have maintained their purchasing power throughout history when monetary systems collapsed precisely because they could not be printed into existence. The world has seen many instances of wars, dictatorships, political revolutions, collapsing currencies, hyperinflation, depressions and more … and throughout them all gold and silver have continued to hold their value.

No one knows when the dollar will decline, the global debt bubble will burst, the dollar loses its reserve currency status, the Petrodollar goes away, or our own fiat currency system collapses but indeed they one day will. It is not a question of *if* but of *when* the era of Bankism blows up. Gold and silver are the insurance policy one holds against those events and other calamities that might one day severely shake the financial system. They are what you buy and store away for your household and children.

When the dust all clears after a period of severe financial trouble, then at the end of the day gold and silver have always retained some sort of value in the new world while other assets have been thoroughly destroyed. Often they even enable you to buy up assets on the cheap whenever a crisis reaches its end.

Remember that people commonly buy insurance policies, even though the probability of accidents is low, because the benefits of having insurance *far outweigh the costs*. This is a common thing to do and no one generally thinks much about it.

Holding gold and silver in your portfolio, instead of just holding paper assets, is like having an insurance policy for troubles in the financial system. In particular, you should especially think of them as a form of insurance *against central bank imprudence* since central bankers, with their unlimited money printing policies, are the root seeds behind financial destruction.

Basically, gold and silver are a protection against monetary recklessness and fiscal foolishness. They have always been the premier investments when governments were acting fiscally or monetarily bizarre. If history does in fact repeat itself, the cost of this form of financial insurance may one day be tremendously cheap in relation to the wealth it could preserve. Hence, while gold and silver are often a "great investment" for reasons of supply and demand imbalances, as with normal commodities, you should also think of holding some precious metals not because they will go up in value but because they are a basic protection against the possibility of extreme financial outcomes.

Right now there are such low yields on U.S. bank deposits, Treasury bonds and Treasury bills that the opportunity cost of owning gold and silver is essentially nil. Because of legal changes in the U.S. even holding cash in a bank now subjects you to financial risks that never existed previously so the metals shouldn't be pariahs. This is because you have now become an "unsecured creditor" to the bank and your funds can be taken if the bank goes under. In other countries your bank deposits entail the risks of bail-ins that might also result in your cash disappearing. That cannot happen if you own physical gold or silver in your possession.

Because people all over are finally waking up and clearly recognizing these risks, this is a major reason why we are seeing fresh money – especially from Asia - buy physical gold and silver as a safety hedge of financial insurance and safe haven investment. This Russian, Chinese, Indian and southeast Asian demand cumulatively far outstrips all available mine supply already!

I believe that we are near one of those historical inflection points that will eventually require a re-juggling of the world's financial system. China, Russia and other nations are trying to replace the predominance of the dollar in world trade, which may ultimately threaten its reserve currency status in time. China is making moves to make oil sales transacted through gold, which would kill the Petrodollar in short order. Using North Korea as an excuse, the U.S. is threatening to block China from US dollar payment systems. At the same time, excessive government debts and QE monetary policies by central banks, overleveraged and undercapitalized banks, and excessive derivative trades and swap agreements have reached levels that now threaten the world's financial system in total. The pot is getting ready to boil over.

Right now the US dollar may seem strong but in terms of fundamentals it is actually weak. Because many nations are starting to trade oil using other currencies, they are abandoning the usage of the dollar (Petrodollar), and hence trillions in dollar-based oil derivative contracts are presently being unwound around the world. Dollar demand is deteriorating so the dollar will decline.

The dollar is seeing competition and replacement that will only accelerate, eventually leading to terrible economic problems such as gross inflation in the United States. As demand for the Petrodollar is fractured, the Saudis and other nations will no doubt dump their dollars and Treasury bonds to buy gold and other stable currencies instead. King Dollar will no longer sit on the throne.

Bankism is part of a larger set of problems that have brought us to this extreme, but one of its most main components. At the present time it is probably prudent to become a gold and silver investor in some measure to protect yourself from the results of Bankism and other misguided government policies that have destroyed the economy and imperiled the financial system. You must prepare yourself for financial crisis because it has happened in the past and it is actually unfolding right now. Events are unfolding exactly along the lines that show the dollar will lose its dominance in world trade, and its banking reserve status may possibly be imperiled. Those ramifications will affect the price of gold and silver.

Furthermore, the odds clearly and strongly favor something going badly wrong in the world's economic, financial and banking conditions – an unforeseen "black swan" event causing contagion is likely to occur - and precious metals are the one form of insurance that could protect you against any unforeseen calamities. Faith in gold and silver usually rises as instability increases.

Thus it is probably prudent for you to hold some gold and silver in your portfolio, and have some Bitcoin as a standby (as an anti- dollar trade), as insurance against the extremes of Bankism.

APPENDIX 1:
SURVIVAL ITEMS DURING
FINANCIAL CRISES

Preppers often make lists of the best barter or survival items to stockpile for emergencies, and these are some of the items that appear most often on these lists:

- ammunition (and guns)
- garden seeds
- candles
- batteries
- solar battery recharger and solar batteries (rechargeable batteries)
- flashlights (and LED headlamps)
- soap
- bleach and detergent
- toilet paper and Kleenex tissue
- diapers
- condoms
- contraceptives
- tampons and pads (feminine products)

- disposable razors and Gilette disposable razor blades
- toiletries (toothpaste, dental floss, shampoo)
- lighters and matches (fire making supplies)
- tobacco and cigarettes
- painkillers (aspirin)
- antibiotics
- bandages
- alcohol and drinking alcohol (wine, beer, liquor)
- screws and nails
- tools (saw blades, hatchets, axe heads, hammer heads, hand drills)
- duct tape
- vitamins
- water and water containers
- fuel (gas, diesel, propane, kerosene)
- reading glasses
- bags
- tie wraps
- fishing supplies
- knives of various sorts
- spices (including salt and pepper)
- sugar
- flour
- rice
- cooking oil
- milk powder
- beans
- dried pasta
- ghee
- chocolate
- coffee and tea
- canned meat (tuna, SPAM, etc.)

- costume jewelry (for trade during occupations)
- cosmetics
- liquor and wine
- playing cards
- pencils, pens and paper
- pepper spray
- mylar and wool blankets
- shoes
- tents
- sewing and mending supplies

Some of the other items people have mentioned include false book safes, small silver coins, nicorette gum, citric acid for canning, rennet tablets for cheese making, baby food, moth balls, winter scarves and gloves, slingshots and ammo, measuring spoons and cups, stovetop waffle makers, basic wound care, eyeglass repair kits, candle molds, Goo Gone goo remover, and windup clocks.

Remember that the official recommendation for water storage is one gallon per person per day. For water filters, many manufacturers are fine such as Berkey and Katadyne (or even the LifeStraw). Experts also recommend that for emergencies you should hold two weeks of deep pantry supplies for the mouths in your home, or one month of food storage per person per household. The serious items in a crisis are always water, food, shelter, clothing, security, medical, transportation, communication and sanitation.

First aid kits should contain additional supplies of Tefla pads that are an improvement over gauze pads since they don't stick to wounds. They should contain Steri-strips, which can close wounds that would otherwise require stitches.

Emergency cash kept on hand should be about one month's of expenses.

APPENDIX 2:
POINTERS FOR ECONOMIC
DEVELOPMENT

Where it was once much easier, with the revamping of the financial system and loss of domestic jobs the challenge of reindustrialization and economic development is sure to confront America in the coming decades. To chart the course ahead we must look to the past and see what worked.

The key to a country becoming rich is not to concentrate on exporting commodities and raw materials since you can't establish a monopoly on them. Instead you are held hostage to world prices. Instead you must point the economy in directions that go up the value chain such as by concentrating on manufacturing. Statesmen who will define U.S. policy in the future need to understand this principle.

What do you then do? I like the rule of brevity exemplified by Winston Churchill, who once wrote the following letter to the First Lord of the Admiralty: "Pray state this day, on one side of a sheet of paper, how the Royal Navy is being adapted to meet the conditions of modern warfare."

One of the best short guides to the principles of national economic prosperity we must use to reboot ourselves comes from *How Rich Countries Got Rich ... And Why Poor Countries Stay Poor*, Erik Reinert, (Carroll & Graf Publishers, New York, 2007), pp. 313-315). Worthy of study, the following list from the book is Philipp von Hornigk's "Nine Points on How to Emulate the Rich Countries (1684)," which illuminates the path of development up the value chain:

First, to inspect the country's soil with the greatest care, and not to leave the agricultural possibilities of a single corner or clod of earth unconsidered. Every useful form of *plant* under the sun should be experimented with, to see whether it is adapted to the country, for the distance or nearness of the sun is not all that counts. Above all, no trouble or expense should be spared to discover gold and silver.

Second, all commodities found in a country, which cannot be used in their natural state, should be worked up within the country; since the payment for *manufacturing* generally exceeds the value of the raw material by two, three, ten, twenty, and even a hundred-fold, and the neglect of this is an abomination to prudent managers.

Third, for carrying out the above two rule, there will be need of people, both for producing and cultivating the raw materials and for working them up. Therefore, attention should be given to the population, that it may be as large as the country can support, this being a well-ordered state's most important concern, but, unfortunately, one that is often neglected. And the people should be turned by all possible means from idleness to remunerative *professions*; instructed and encouraged in all kinds of *inventions*, arts and trades; and, if necessary, instructors should be brought in from foreign countries for this.

Fourth, gold and silver once in the country, whether

from its own mines or obtained by *industry* from foreign countries, are under no circumstances to be taken out for any purpose, so far as possible, or be allowed to be buried in chests or coffers, but must always remain in *circulation*; nor should much be permitted in uses where they are at once *destroyed* and cannot be utilized again. For under these conditions, it will be impossible for a country that has once acquired a considerable supply of cash, especially one that possesses gold and silver mines, ever to sink into poverty; indeed, it is impossible that it should not continually increase in wealth and property. Therefore,

Fifth, the inhabitants of the country should make every effort to get along with their domestic products, to confine their luxury to these alone, and to do without foreign products as far as possible (except where great need leaves no alternative, or if not need, widespread, unavoidable abuse, of which the Indian spices are an example). And so on,

Sixth, in case the said purchases were indispensible because of necessity or *irremediable* abuse, they should be obtained from these foreigners at first hand, so far as possible, and not for gold or silver, but in exchange for other domestic wares.

Seventh, such foreign commodities should in this case be imported in unfinished form, and worked up within the country, thus earning the wages of *manufacturing there.*

Eighth, opportunities should be sought night and day for selling the country's superfluous goods to these foreigners in manufactured form, so far as this is necessary, and for gold and silver; and to this end, *consumption*, so to speak, must be sought in the farthest ends of the earth, and developed in every possible way.

Ninth, except for important considerations, no importation should be allowed under any circumstances of commodities of which there is a sufficient supply of suitable quality at home; and in this matter neither sympathy nor compassion should be shown foreigners, be they friends, kinsfolk, *allies* or enemies. For all friendship ceases, when it involves my weakness and ruin. And this holds good, even if the domestic commodities are of poorer quality, or even higher priced. For it would be better to pay for an article two dollars which remains in the country than only which goes out, however strange this may seem to the ill-informed.

The next instructive list is Kishore Mahbubani's "Ten Commandments for Developing Countries in the Nineties" taken from *Can Asians Think?*, Kishore Mahbubani, (Times Book International, Singapore, 2002, pp. 190-191):

1.   Thou shalt blame only thyself for thy failures in development. Blaming imperialism, colonialism, and neo-imperialism is a convenient excuse to avoid self-examination.
2.   Thou shalt acknowledge that corruption is the single most important cause of failures in development. Developed countries are not free from corruption, but with their affluence they can afford to indulge in savings and loan scandals.
3.   Thou shalt not subsidize any product, nor punish the farmer in order to favor the city dweller. High prices are the only effective signal to increase production. If there are food riots, thou shalt resign from office.
4.   Thou shalt abandon state control for free markets. Thou shalt have faith in thine own population. An alive and productive population naturally causes development.
5.   Thou shalt borrow no more. Thou shalt get foreign investment that pays for itself. Thou shalt build only the infrastructure that is needed and create no white elephants or railways that end in deserts. Thou shalt accept no aid that is intended only to subsidize ailing industries in developed countries.
6.   Thou shalt not reinvent the wheel. Millions of people

have gone through the path of development. Take the well-traveled roads. Be not prisoners of dead ideologies.

7. Thou shalt scrub the ideas of Karl Marx out of thy mind and replace them with the ideas of Adam Smith. The Germans have made their choice. Thou shalt follow suit.

8. Thou shalt be humble when developing and not lecture the developed world on their sins. They listened politely in the 1960s and 1970s. They no longer will in the 1990s.

9. Thou shalt abandon all North-South forums, which only encourage hypocritical speeches and token gestures. Thou shalt remember that the countries that have received the greatest amount of aid per capita have failed most spectacularly in development. Thou shalt throw out all theories of development.

10. Thou shalt not abandon hope. People are the same the world over. What Europe achieved yesterday, the developing world will achieve tomorrow. It can be done.

Both of these lists should be studied by politicians and policy initiators who wish to become true statesmen. This mindset can lay the development course for the nation.

Along these lines the last list to reference, drawn up by economic historian David Landes (taken from Niall Ferguson's *Empire: The Rise and Demise of the British World Order and the Lessons for Global Power*, p. 307), includes the measures that an "ideal growth-and-development" government should adopt:

- Secure rights of private property, the better to encourage saving and investment;
- Secure rights of personal liberty ... against both the abuses of tyranny and ... crime and corruption;
- Enforce rights of contract;
- Provide stable government ... governed by publicly known rules;
- Provide responsive government;

- Provide honest government ... (with) no rents to favour and position;
- Provide moderate, efficient, ungreedy government ... to hold taxes down (and) reduce the government's claim on the social surplus.

Going forwards, all countries must keep these principles in mind when undertaking industrialization, financial, economic and other development efforts for their nation.

ABOUT THE AUTHOR

Bill Bodri is an ex-Wall Streeter and popular author of investment and business books including:

- *Breakthrough Strategies of Wall Street Traders: 17 Remarkable Traders Reveal Their Top Performing Investment Strategies*

- *Super Investing: 5 Proven Methods for Beating the Market and Retiring Rich*

- *Move Forward: Powerful Strategies for Creating Better Outcomes in Life*

- *Quick, Fast, Done: Simple Time Management Secrets From Some of History's Greatest Leaders*

If you enjoyed this book you would probably enjoy *Super Investing* since it covers similar themes. *Breakthrough Strategies of Wall Street Traders* contains proprietary trading and investing methods that several Wall Street millionaires used to make their riches and is similar in content to *Market Wizards*.

The author can be reached for interviews through wbodri@gmail.com.

www.ingramcontent.com/pod-product-compliance
Lightning Source LLC
Chambersburg PA
CBHW070729220326
41598CB00024BA/3358